THE HEART
OF
WORK

THE
HEART

of
WORK

10 KEYS TO LIVING YOUR CALLING

RYUHO OKAWA

IRH Press

Okawa Books is an imprint of IRH Press USA Inc.
IRH PRESS
New York

Library of Congress Cataloging-in-Publication Data

ISBN 13: 978-1-942125-03-7
ISBN 10: 1-942125-03-8

Printed in China
First edition

Cover Designer: Karla Baker
Cover/Interior Image © Berezina/Shutterstock.com

Contents

~ CHAPTER 1 ~
Finding the True Essence of Work

~ CHAPTER 2 ~
Accomplishing Outstanding Work

Preface to the Current Edition

Ever since the first Japanese edition of this book was published in March 1990, it has found an eager readership throughout the business community, from young executives in their twenties and thirties to directors and corporate magnates.

At the same time, the business environment has undergone drastic changes over recent years. This has led to a growing sense of uncertainty about the future and an increasing demand for clear guidelines for succeeding at work. I have decided to publish the revised edition of this book under a new title in the hope that it will reach the many people who are in search of such guidelines.

This book outlines a philosophy of work that I have developed at my organization, Happy Science. It is my sincere hope that a greater number of people will learn and master this philosophy of work and that this book will help them achieve true success.

Ryuho Okawa
Founder and CEO
Happy Science Group

Preface to the Original Edition

In October 1989, I published *Invincible Thinking*, which, to my delight, was very well received throughout the country and became a best-selling title with hundreds of thousands of copies sold. But since this book presented guidelines and principles on life in general, I have received numerous requests from people in the business community asking for more practical and concrete guidelines for approaching and succeeding at work.

In response to their enthusiasm, I have decided to put together my fragmented thoughts on the philosophy of work that I have developed over the course of years and publish them as a book. Although it was not possible for me to cover every facet of business in a single book, I have discussed topics that continue to fascinate me, such as the true essence of work, how to do outstanding work, conditions for climbing the ladder of success, and a completely new perspective on the relationship between work and the spirit of love.

Those of you who live your work every day will make new discoveries about the meaning of work as you read the pages that follow. You can start reading this book from chapter one, as we usually do when we're reading, but you can also start from the chapter that interests you the most. No matter where you start, I'm sure you will find hints to success in life throughout the book. I hope this book will help you find the path that will lead you to achieve your dreams.

I recommend that you read this book not only once, but twice or three times. It will not only help you become successful in the business world, but will also let you race ahead on the golden road to success in life.

Ryuho Okawa
Founder and CEO
Happy Science Group

CHAPTER 1

FINDING *the* TRUE ESSENCE *of* WORK

❦ 1 ❦
THE HUMAN NATURE OF WORK

Most of us feel that it's only natural to work. Finding a career is part of becoming a full member of society, which we expect to do after we graduate from school. Even seven-year-olds expect to get a job when they grow up, and they know that the money they earn from working will pay the bills for necessities and leisure activities.

From a relatively young age, we see our lives as divided into two periods. We spend the first period of life building ourselves—cultivating skills and developing our character. During this time, we usually don't receive any compensation or get paid for what we do. Our main focus, especially in our school days, is studying and perhaps building physical strength. This is a time when we are financially dependent on our parents.

In the latter period, we go out into the world and get a job. Our task now is to produce something of benefit to the world and get paid or compensated for what we do. We not only earn our living, but also provide for our family so that our children can now cultivate skills and build themselves without having to worry about making a living. There are, of course, exceptions, so we cannot always make such a clear-cut distinction between these two periods of life. For example, some mothers return to work after giving birth, while others become stay-at-home moms, and a lot of students take on part-time jobs to support their family. But whatever our occupation is, work is a fundamental part of life.

To understand the role of work in your life, consider the following question: How often do you feel grateful that you have work to do? If you ever feel discontented with your work, have you stopped to consider what it would be like to live without any work to do? You can probably imagine yourself getting bored pretty quickly.

Of course, there are people like Bodhidharma, a Buddhist monk who introduced Zen Buddhism to China. He is said to have sat facing a wall for nine years without speaking to anyone. He probably didn't earn any money facing a wall, but his dedication to the practice of Zen served as a model of spiritual discipline for the Zen Buddhists that followed him. If a non-practitioner sat in front of a wall for nine years, he would no doubt be ridiculed and criticized for not doing anything at all or for not providing for his family.

We human beings are not made to just sit around and do nothing at all. We are imbued with a desire to work. This aptitude is something we are born with, not something we acquire later in life. It is a fundamental part of being human. Some animals work, in the sense that they exert themselves to survive, but, unlike humans, animals cannot break away from a fixed pattern of activities. Let me explain this using some examples.

Sea otters have complex feeding habits that are quite advanced for an animal. They dive to capture shellfish from the ocean floor, then swim back and eat them on the ocean surface while floating on their back. They put the shellfish on their bellies and use "tools" such as rocks to crack open the shells. They may look as if they are working on a specific task, but in fact they are simply using a conventional method of feeding themselves. They are just doing what sea otters do. But they never take on new tasks. Sea otters don't, for example, develop new methods of getting food or cook the shellfish they've caught.

The same holds true for other animals. For instance, sheep grow fleece, and from our perspective, that is their job. A sheep's fleece can be used for a multitude of purposes, but I doubt that sheep are aware of the purpose for growing fleece. It is something that they do naturally; they don't make a conscious effort to produce good fleece for the market. Chickens lay eggs, but they do not produce anything out of the eggs. They do not cook eggs, nor do they trade their eggs for something else; they only engage in a set pattern of behavior.

The work that we humans do is quite different in nature. We all have the ability to create something new using the unique talents that each of us has. We are capable of producing a variety of objects from a single material. We are in a blessed position to feel the same sense of joy that the Primordial God of the Great Universe experienced at the time of Creation.

The essence of work is very closely related to the nature of human beings. God gave us the desire to work so that He could share His joy of Creation with us.

❧ 2 ❧

THE REWARDS OF WORK

When God gave us work, He made sure that it didn't end there. He made it so that we get rewarded for good work. In most cases, this reward takes the form of monetary compensation or career advancement. It can also be a spiritual joy that comes from receiving compliments from a lot of people.

God could have made a system in which we would exert ourselves to work regardless of whether we would be rewarded, but He decided to let us receive compensation for our efforts. He knew that this was the key that would allow human beings to keep working forever. What if God had set a rule that the chefs in upscale restaurants were only allowed to prepare exquisite cuisine for the customers and were never allowed to enjoy that cuisine themselves? After a while, great chefs would find it difficult to continue in their profession, master culinary arts, and feel proud of their work.

We are motivated to refine and improve our skills because we are rewarded for good work. This may sound like a selfish idea, but it really isn't. Behind this idea is God's grand plan. He created a system, out of mercy, that allows us to savor the joy of work forever.

Our work is always rewarded—but the reward may not necessarily be monetary. Sometimes, we are rewarded with a good family, a fine house, financial stability, or the freedom to try new ventures. Good work can also lead to the good opinion of others, self-improvement, and higher social status. Whatever their form, good work always brings in rewards.

In essence, the nature of work is to produce value. Good work is activity that creates benefits. We are compensated for our work because our actions create some kind of profit. We feel guilty for getting paid when our actions have inconvenienced others or damaged the company, because we are receiving a reward even though our work has had a negative effect. Conversely, we are not surprised when even promising workers are demoted, face a pay cut, or, in the worst scenario, lose their job, if their actions have harmed the company. The work we do is supposed to create value and bring in profits, and that's why we are rewarded for it. We should be grateful for receiving compensation for our work, but at the same time, this system was designed by God, so it is only natural.

We should dedicate our lives to our work, because when we do, we experience the reward of spiritual joy. By contrast, when we work half-heartedly, we feel a twinge of conscience or emptiness; we sense that something is not right.

You may have heard a story about a prodigal heir who destroyed his family's wealth and position after he inherited a vast amount of money from his parents or took over the family business. In many versions of this story, the cause of the son's failure is his inability to devote his life to work; as a result, he feels empty inside. He tries to fill in the gap and gloss over his inability to work by immersing himself in the pursuit of pleasure, spending money lavishly until he finds himself bankrupt. People in this situation share a feeling of guilt for receiving compensation for work that they haven't staked their lives on. They try to stave off this guilt by fooling themselves; they stop thinking rationally and take on strange ventures to numb their senses.

When we look out at the world, we see that those who stake their lives on their work rarely fail. Even Jesus Christ, who did not gain high social status or achieve financial success despite having completely devoted his life to his mission, was rewarded in the end. Jesus has been venerated and worshipped as the lord of humankind for two thousand years, and this itself represents a tremendous reward for his work. The work we devote our life to will never go unrewarded, and when we receive this reward with gratitude, our soul will fill with joy.

❀ 3 ❀

THREE STEPS
TO DEVOTING YOUR LIFE TO WORK

Step 1 Discover Your Calling

How can we devote our lives to work? The first step, before anything else, is to find our calling. It is very difficult to devote our life to our work unless we feel that it is our vocation.

For example, no matter how well-built a person may be, he will find it hard to imagine himself becoming a baseball player or a professional wrestler if all he is interested in is studying. If his soul finds delight in a life of study and wants to pursue an academic path, his physical aptitude will not make it any easier for him to dedicate his life to wrestling or baseball.

Although finding our calling is the prerequisite to devoting our life to work, a lot of people in the world today, especially those who are doing office work, probably find it difficult to find their calling in their current job. If you feel that you haven't yet found your vocation, don't lose hope. You may be able to find a vocation by changing your career, so I recommend that you concentrate on finding a job that you feel is your calling. If you can believe that you've discovered your calling in your job—that it is your mission—then you will be able to devote your entire life to your work.

I emphasize the importance of finding our calling because when we do, we're already halfway toward fulfilling our mission in life. It doesn't matter how talented or untalented we feel we are. If we want to achieve great success in life, we need to find a job that we believe is our calling.

Even the most talented painters will not be successful if they're limited to doing clerical work. In the same way, the talents of gifted scientists cannot blossom if they are trained to be poets. Everybody has a place where their unique gifts can bloom. The important thing is to search and find the job for which we are best suited.

Step 2 Develop a Zest for Work

The second and most important step to dedicating our life to work is to have enthusiasm. There are a lot of smart people in this world, but not all of them have achieved outstanding success. I had always wondered why some very intelligent people are not able to show their abilities, get paid well, or get ahead at work. So I decided to carefully watch and study some of these people. After a while, I came to the conclusion that they lacked enthusiasm. Even the brightest among us cannot improve our work skills or open up new paths unless we are enthusiastic about what we do.

What do you think is the most critical element in making good pottery? Even if we have the best skills, the best clay, the best glaze, and the best design, we will not be able to produce the final product without firing it in a kiln. The fire in the kiln is equivalent to our enthusiasm for work. Without enthusiasm, we cannot produce first-class results, even if we have the best talents, best skills, and best ideas.

Jesus Christ was able to accomplish so much because he had passion for his mission. The same is true of Socrates. He was an exceptionally intelligent person, but that alone isn't what made him a leading historical figure. The only reason his name remains known to this day is that he was enthusiastic about his work. Confucius's passion was the driving force that kept him going as he traveled around the country preaching. Shakyamuni Buddha was able to preach and leave behind an immense number of versatile teachings about the Truths because he was passionate about his mission. Shakyamuni was very intelligent, as is reflected in the old Eastern expression, "smart like Shakyamuni." But in the end, it was his enthusiasm that made Shakyamuni carry out his mission.

No matter how exceptional our talents are, we

will go unnoticed unless we bring them out into the world. Our enthusiasm is what makes our gifts blossom and sparkle. To be successful, we may need brains or brawn, but our zealous enthusiasm is what will lead us to success in the end.

Conversely, a lack of enthusiasm will prevent us from excelling. This principle applies not only to work we are paid for, but also to unpaid work. Only when homemakers manage the household with enthusiasm can they successfully support bread-winners' devotion to their paid work. On the other hand, if homemakers are apathetic instead of passionate about their work, they make it more difficult for breadwinners to achieve great success. Imagine soldiers going to war. They cannot fight well if their armor is coming apart and their swords are rusty. Someone needs to make sure that they have everything they need before they set out to war.

I can't emphasize this too much: zeal is the jewel that surpasses everything else in any effort to achieve success.

Step 3 Fill Your Heart with Gratitude

The third step to devoting our life to work is to understand that some of the workings of the world remain invisible to the human eye. Some people may think that this idea is old-fashioned or superstitious, but it is the truth.

There are millions of companies in the world. In Japan alone, there are at least a few million companies. Many of these companies run at a loss or barely break even and have just enough cash to pay the employees. But some of these businesses outperform others by far, develop into corporate giants, and expand globally.

What is the secret to their success? Of course, it could be the diligent work of each of the employees. Still, I cannot help but sense that, above all, the turning of fortune's wheel is at work. Whether we're talking about a person or a corporation, I believe that the workings of good fortune are behind every success.

What, then, can we do to encourage the invisible power of good fortune to help us? First, we must believe in our own luck. And to believe in our luck, it's essential to feel that God protects us and rejoices in our work. If you find that *God* is too big to think about, try imagining how your ancestors or the founder or previous CEOs of your company would feel if they looked at your work. Do you feel a sense of joy and blessing coming from them? That feeling is essential to attracting good fortune.

Many companies start to decline after the fourth or fifth generation of owners because the current owner neglects to appreciate the efforts of the previous owners. When the owner forgets the original purpose of the company and no longer feels grateful to those who built the basis for the current prosperity, the owner's luck begins to falter, and the company starts doing poorly.

Receiving guidance from God or heavenly spirits is essential to a life dedicated to work. Only when we believe that we are doing a job that is blessed by heaven will we be able to devote our life to it. Receiving blessings and divine support will improve our luck, and a path to success will open before us.

Having faith in God—or, in other words, being grateful to the Source or Higher Power—is fundamental to doing great work. A willingness to serve a greater purpose and a devotion to God are what make it possible for us to dedicate our life to our calling.

Our success depends on our gratitude and devotion to something greater than ourselves. People who are intelligent but do not achieve success behave like critics and find fault with others, but they lack gratitude or enthusiasm for their work. Gratitude to God is the driving force behind enthusiasm. It is a pity that some people ridicule those who work with gratitude to God. We should not let their sneering bother us; instead, we should stay grateful and keep working diligently to achieve success.

We should dedicate our heart and soul to work. Work is what we devote our entire life to. When we find our calling, work with passion, and move forward with the guidance of heaven, we will be walking on the path to spiritual success.

CHAPTER 2

ACCOMPLISHING OUTSTANDING WORK

1

THE FIRST KEY

IDENTIFYING YOUR CORE MISSION AND OBJECTIVES

L et's say that now we know what we were born to do. Our hearts are burning with wholehearted enthusiasm for dedicating our lives to this calling. So how do we do it? How do we go about living our calling and achieving what we are meant for in life?

In this chapter, I will be explaining how to cultivate the three keys to doing outstanding work. There are such a variety of walks of life that it is impossible to offer a work philosophy that would be universal to everyone. But businesspeople may especially appreciate the habits I discuss here, and people in other trades and professions will also be able to get full use out of them as they work to fulfill their calling.

The first key, which is especially important to businesspeople, is to develop a habit of grasping your job's core purpose as quickly as possible. Different people take different amounts of time to develop a good understanding of their job's core purpose, and how long it takes to come to this understanding is more a matter of personality than a measure of ability. Some of us are capable of catching on quickly, say in a day, while others may take as long as six months.

The person who catches on quickly does not necessarily have superior ability—over the long term, either one may be able to achieve great success. But as worker mobility improves and society becomes more competitive, there will be increasing pressure to understand our core responsibilities quickly. We can do this by dividing them into three key goals: our big objective, our medium-sized objective, and our small objectives. As career changes become more frequent, the key to a businessperson's success is being conscientious of these three sets of objectives.

The big objective of your work is the chief mission that your company is trying to achieve. You can significantly improve your chances of success by making an effort to quickly grasp your company's core objective, main operations, key characteristics, and specific type of enterprise. Every industry and type of enterprise has a chief mission that defines it. For example, a real estate company's mission is to sell property. A manufacturer's purpose is to produce goods. A financial institution is a business that offers financial services. And a trading company trades international goods.

When we have understood our company's chief role in society, we are ready to determine our department's role in reaching that goal. We want to gain a clear understanding of what our department does. Our department's role is our work's medium-sized objective. Finally, to understand our job's small objectives, we want to get down to the specific responsibilities that we have been assigned and everything that they entail, and then think of what they mean in the scheme of things.

It is especially important to understand the big, medium-sized, and small purposes of our responsibilities as quickly as possible when we are succeeding into someone else's job. We can easily fall behind if we focus only on finding out what our predecessor did without considering what it all means in the general scheme of things, with the expectation that we will learn more as we go. Since we may have to learn a different way of working than we are used to when we transition into a new company, missing the bigger purpose could make us susceptible to making large mistakes. But if we create a habit of identifying our big objective, medium-sized objective, and small objectives from the beginning, we will find it easier to thoroughly understand our new job's chief mission and framework, and we will adapt well to our new working environment. This habit will make us outstanding workers.

～ ∂ 2 ∂ ～
THE SECOND KEY
PRIORITIZING

T he second key to successful work is setting priorities. If we created a detailed list of all the
tasks and responsibilities that we carry out during
a typical workday, week, or month, we would probably end up listing over a hundred tasks, and we may
likely find that we are carrying out many of these
tasks routinely, without thinking about whether
these tasks are truly important. So, especially when
you are starting a new job, it is very important to
start each day by reviewing your tasks. The key is
to figure out all the jobs that you are being assigned
and then rank them in order of importance.

Develop a habit of going through your list of responsibilities and deciding which are the most important,
which are the next most important, and which are
least important. If you have one hundred tasks on

your list, normally only two to three will be of chief importance. About ten or twenty will be second in priority, and the remaining eighty will be necessary but incidental to your most important tasks.

If you ever feel stuck, it may be a sign that you have become lost in a forest of incidental tasks instead of focusing on your chief responsibilities. If you take the task of creating an accounting spreadsheet as an example, it is as if you are spending the majority of your day working out the figures without first getting a grasp of the chart's purpose. This limits you from making more important decisions beyond just punching numbers. In this situation, you need to take a step back from the calculations to imagine the purpose of this spreadsheet. Then you might go another step further, look at your job from a broader perspective, and consider how important this task really is. Sometimes, when we take a broad view like this, we find that some of our routine tasks can be replaced by a more efficient process, and sometimes we find that they can be eliminated altogether because they are no longer necessary.

Sometimes we make the mistake of doing what I call working in reverse: we deplete valuable time by beginning with less-important tasks that end up taking a large part of our time and only working on our core responsibilities later. Instead, we want to begin with the core and work outward. When you realize that you have been overspending your energy on too many peripheral tasks, the first thing to do is determine your most important responsibilities and then identify the secondary tasks that support those responsibilities. Then review those secondary tasks and determine how productive they are. Consider whether you are the right person to carry out those tasks, whether you should delegate them to someone else, or whether to eliminate them completely. If you regularly prioritize and review your responsibilities, you will often notice tasks that you didn't really need to do.

The way to maximize your efficiency is to make a list of all of your tasks and responsibilities and rank them from A to C based on their importance. Once you have finished, review the tasks in the "B" category, followed by the "C" category, based on how much they contribute to fulfilling your "A"-ranked priorities. As you review your list, keep an eye out for any tasks that do not support your chief responsibilities and so might be eliminated. Then decide which tasks to keep on your list of responsibilities and which are less important and should be let go. For example, if you are in a management position, you want to find the tasks that can be eliminated or delegated so you can devote your full time and energy to management-level work.

This working style will also help you decide how you want to tackle your work on a daily basis. We ordinarily have several assignments running simultaneously, and this makes us vulnerable to becoming disorganized and panicking. Prioritizing is especially valuable when you find your day being swamped with too many assignments. The key in this situation is to prioritize by urgency. Identify the jobs that are most urgent to your superior and prioritize the tasks that need to be handled soonest. Quickly determine which tasks need your attention immediately, which can be addressed an hour later, which don't need to be completed until the end of the day, and which you can attend to tomorrow or later. By taking the time to check your priorities daily, you will ensure that you do not slow down other people's work by mistakenly working on assignments that are less urgent to your superior. Mastering the habit of prioritizing will propel you toward becoming an outstanding worker.

※ ～ 3 ～ ※

THE THIRD KEY
NURTURING GOOD RELATIONSHIPS

The third key to becoming an outstanding worker is creating and improving relationships with the people we work with. Nurturing good relationships with our superiors, subordinates, and other colleagues is essential to running our jobs smoothly and achieving results, because work is never accomplished completely by ourselves.

To help us develop good workplace relationships, we can imagine a relationship graph. Not all relationships should be approached the same way, and using a graph to arrange the people you work with into groups gives you a clear guide for sorting out the emotions you may face in relating to different colleagues and determining the best way to engage with everyone.

On the relationship graph, we are standing at

the intersection of the vertical and horizontal axes with people lined up above us, below us, to the right, and to the left. All the people we work with fit into one of the four quadrants on this graph. The first and second quadrants, above us, represent everyone who works in a position above ours, and the third and fourth quadrants include everyone in a position below ours. Colleagues whose rank is similar to ours fall on the horizontal axis. *See figure 1.*

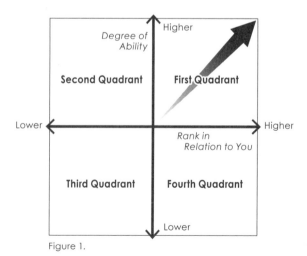

Figure 1.

The upward arrow represents the people we should consider our role models as we strive to advance in the company, and those who are looking to us for leadership are located below the axis. The horizontal axis indicates people's ability and competency. So, the right side of the vertical axis—the first and fourth quadrants—includes everyone we consider to be more capable than ourselves. And those with less ability fall on the left side of the vertical axis, in the second or third quadrants.

We can now consider our graph by quadrant and list the people we work with in their groups: The first quadrant includes people who are in higher positions and are more capable than we are. The second quadrant includes people who rank higher in the company, but whom we may surpass when we reach their age or experience level. The third quadrant is made up of junior colleagues who are not as gifted in ability, and the fourth quadrant is composed of those who are junior and more capable.

Of all the people in your company, the names you

have written down in the first quadrant will have the most influence on your advancement. The key to succeeding in the company is learning from the people in this group, approaching them as role models, and winning their approval.

When we relate to the people in the second quadrant, we want to provide them enough safe space to make sure we do not agitate them. Since the people in this group may feel threatened by our abilities, we should be careful not to psychologically push ahead of them—for example, by creating a sense of pressure on them or by thinking of them as incompetent. Often, demotions are the effects of jealousy and bad-mouthing from people in this group. Within our heart, we should set a respectful distance between where they stand and where we stand. If they are our superiors or the managers of our department, we should treat them with due respect as people in higher positions of responsibility. We need to avoid getting ahead of ourselves and thinking we are their equal or superior in ability. That way, we give them the space to do their job without agitation and ensure that they won't find reason to disturb us as we do our job.

Our relationships with people in the third quadrant are like the relationships between a politician and citizens. The people you assigned to this section are not likely to be major competitors who will get ahead of you. People in this group are well aware that you have superior abilities and are far ahead of them. So their main concern is whether they can trust that following your leadership will lead them to a bright future. As a noble politician would treat his or her beloved people, you will treat people in the third quadrant with warm kindness and whole-hearted sincerity and envelop them with love. It will have a negative effect on your performance if you withdraw them from your team or allow their abilities to be stifled. The work of these employees is indispensable for the smooth running of your job and the company, just as an officer's regiment is crippled without his soldiers. No one would criticize soldiers for lacking the ability to serve as an officer, because that is not their role. Similarly, you are their leader who is responsible for taking care of this group. Give them what they need to work happily and at their best, and envelop them with the generous love that a mother bird would give to her chicks and eggs.

Finally, the people in the fourth quadrant are likely to advance ahead of you in several years' time. They will test your capacity for leadership: you will be challenged to show your ability to lead competent and talented people. Managers who advance are skillful at finding outstanding people to work for them to achieve excellent results. For example, the ability to skillfully command a group of outstanding soldiers is considered the hallmark of an excellent general.

The key is not to give in to jealousy. You should keep a big heart: praise their talents and give them the support they need to grow further. By acknowledging their abilities and giving them the recognition they deserve, you will create a strong relationship of trust. People with exceptional abilities will work hard and sacrifice for someone who recognizes their strengths. In a military scenario, this trust develops into the kind of devotion that leads soldiers to risk their lives for the general. In a company scenario, this trust develops into dedicated effort to help your work succeed and to contribute to your advancement.

It is impossible to succeed and advance at anything all on your own. It is vital to your success to have a big enough heart to take many talented people under your wings and gain their support and commitment. Then, leave the rest of your future up to heaven, and do not worry about what may happen when they advance ahead of you. If it happens, it happens. You will be ready to accept whatever fate holds for you. But as long as you are their superior, you will devote everything you have to extracting every ounce of their abilities to the fullest.

As you work to develop good relationships, you should start to see your position in your workplace rising at a forty-five-degree angle into the first quadrant. You will continue along this course and gradually climb your way to the highest point, on the right-hand corner. This process is also a way to be an outstanding worker.

Once we have these three keys, the next step toward outstanding work is learning to approach our job with a strategic mindset. First, we need to set a large goal. Then we develop a plan, including a detailed list of actions indicating how we will carry out our plan and what kind of ideas we need to achieve our goal. Taking these steps will guarantee your further advancement.

CHAPTER 3

CLIMBING
the LADDER *of*
SUCCESS

1
WHAT IS CAREER SUCCESS?

We all want to achieve great things in our work and be recognized for our achievements. And the recognition we gain leads us to a higher position in society. This is what we often refer to as *success*. For corporate workers, promotions usually make success easy to measure. Entrepreneurs and CEOs can use the development of their businesses to gauge their success. For writers, success comes when their work becomes a best-selling book, which gives them social dignity, status, and fame. The magnitude of change that they go through can be compared with an office assistant suddenly becoming an executive manager.

Success can come in different forms in different areas of life. You may achieve great things in fields outside of your work—for example, you may be awarded an honorary post in the local council. In academics, the qualifications you receive, a doctorate for example, may build up your position and become the measure of success in your career. Receiving a degree from an acclaimed university can also be a form of success.

Those of us who live in a constitutional country are guaranteed equal opportunity. This means that we can choose the school we wish to attend, the career we wish to pursue, and the way of life we wish to lead, regardless of whether we were born rich or poor and what our parents' occupations are. This freedom of choice gives rise to free competition, which brings success to some individuals. In the process of walking on the path to success, we learn from each other and improve ourselves. Some climb up the ladder of success, while others stumble along the way.

Generally, we think of success as something that's recognized in this world. This is true to a certain extent, but we can also achieve success in the inner world. Even if we don't attain a high status in society, we can still cultivate a very rich heart. From a spiritual point of view, it is definitely a form of success to leave this world with a higher state of mind than you entered it with. In fact, I have explored this topic in many of my other books, so in this chapter, I would like to focus on career advancement, a type of success that involves receiving recognition in the material world.

2

THE FIRST CONDITION
FOR A SUCCESSFUL CAREER
FIND JOY IN WORKING

The first condition for climbing the ladder of success may seem obvious: hard work. If you picked up this book expecting to learn a secret of success that allows you to avoid hard work, you may be disappointed. But although successful people are not always aware of this, the primary things that have led to their success are that they enjoy working and they work to the full extent of their abilities.

Even if we get a stroke of pure luck, it will only bring us temporary success, not lasting success, because this sort of success is not something we have used our abilities to achieve. To illustrate this, let's say that a student sneaks into the faculty room and peeks at the exam. Even if the student scores high on the exam, it will not benefit him in the long run. Or you could get lucky on a test: the test could include questions that you already know the answers to. But luck on that one test will not guarantee that you will pass a university admissions test. The same kind of thing is true outside of school, in the working world, and in every walk of life.

Life in the real world is like a duel with real swords. During your apprenticeship, you train using bamboo swords, but that training alone does not prepare you to win a fight with a real sword. In a practice session with a bamboo sword, you need to strike a clear blow to gain a point. But in a real sword fight, a glancing stroke of the tip of the sword could do enough damage to win the match. Fighting with a real sword tests your true ability. Even if you learn to use elaborate techniques with a practice sword, these skills will be useless unless you can draw on them in a real fight.

What I am trying to illustrate is that, no matter how much time you spend devising methodologies and strategies and acquiring knowledge, this alone will not prove your ability in the real world. To prove your ability at work, you need to love working in the first place because only hardworking people can improve their abilities in their work. This may sound like a hard truth, but this is something that we should take to heart if we want to be successful.

Do you know how many paintings an artist needs to paint before she turns out a masterpiece? She paints thousands, if not tens of thousands, of canvases to create a work of genius. If she has to paint ten thousand paintings to create that one masterpiece, would you say that the previous 9,999 paintings were entirely in vain? Probably not. All her work on those paintings developed her gift. The final masterpiece is a reward for all the hard work she put into getting to that point.

As you can see, finding joy and purpose in work is the first condition for success. The reward for your work is the joy and fulfillment you feel from working. Once you reach a state of simply enjoying working, you'll never want to give it up; your eyes will be filled with excitement when you get to work, and work will become the source of your happiness.

Have you ever deeply contemplated the importance of a sense of fulfillment in your work? When your work fulfills you, you feel filled with joy when, at the end of the day or throughout the year, you reflect on the good work you have done. This joy surpasses all other feelings of pleasure. Some may say they find more pleasure in leisure activities, such as gambling and sports, than in their work, but I believe that these people have never tasted the fulfillment that comes from working hard. In a sense, they are looking for pleasure elsewhere because they have yet to discover the true joy that work brings. This tendency can be likened to that of a man who is never satisfied with the love he receives from a woman he loves, or a woman who feels that she is not loved enough by the man she is with. These people may get involved in one love affair after another and keep changing partners to look for that perfect person who can give them all the love they want. But they will never be satisfied as long as they keep searching for pleasure in places other than the place they belong. They need to find and experience the joy in doing what they are supposed to be doing in the first place.

Most of us live a life of seventy to eighty years. When you look back over the years at the end of your life, what do you think will have stayed with you as your most authentic source of joy? It is the sense of fulfillment that will come from all the hard work you have done. This feeling of satisfaction will give you the greatest joy that you can experience. And we can achieve this, not by chance, but by continuing to work. Just as you would need to dig to a certain depth to strike gold in a gold mine, you have to work and cultivate yourself for a number of years to experience the joy of working.

It makes a big difference if you can find your calling or vocation. Some may enjoy working part-time, but they probably do not consider their part-time job to be their vocation. In some cases, part-time jobs offer better pay than full-time jobs. But higher pay alone is not enough to keep us motivated. The true joy of work comes not from monetary compensation, but from something that surpasses it—finding joy in our life.

I believe that we should start with what I consider to be the golden rule for success. The first condition for a successful career is to enjoy working—to find joy in your job. For those who dislike working, true success will be hard to come by. They may become successful for a period of time, but their success will not last long.

3

THE SECOND CONDITION FOR A SUCCESSFUL CAREER
BECOME A USEFUL PERSON

The second condition for climbing the ladder of success is to become someone who is useful or beneficial to the organization or society we belong to. Contrary to common perception, the secret of success is not ability, but usefulness. Can you tell the difference?

A lot of people misunderstand this and believe that it is their ability that will bring them success, recognition, and higher social status. While ability helps to a certain extent, it is usually not enough to ensure success. Success is not necessarily about how much ability you have, but how you make use of your ability within the context of your relationships with others.

To illustrate, let's say that we have a sharp samurai sword. No matter how sharp it is, it will not help someone who is looking for a tool to use to prepare a meal. Imagine wielding a three-foot sword in the kitchen to cut radishes, tomatoes, or onions. While the sword is sharp enough to serve the purpose, its sharpness could also be dangerous to the person using it. Ability can be likened to the sharpness of a sword: it becomes very useful in the right place, but it can be dangerous if handled wrongly. In other words, we become useful and beneficial when we use our ability to help bring profits to the group to which we belong. If, on the other hand, we are working in an environment where our skills are not useful, we will not be able to exercise our abilities, and, in the worst-case scenario, our ability could even cause harm. Once we are aware of this, we need to ascertain what it is that our workplace requires of us—whether it is a razor, scissors, a carving knife, a saw, a hatchet, a sword, or an axe.

For instance, an entry-level employee may have a thorough knowledge of how to manage people. But if he is placed as an office assistant, he will not make use of his knowledge. And if he tries, he could be seen as a nuisance who criticizes his bosses and spreads rumors about his coworkers without doing his own job as an assistant. He may have the potential to become the human resources department director in about twenty years. But his entry-level position may not require this ability. If we want to be successful in our career, we need to know and exercise the ability required by our current position.

I would like to emphasize that life does not require just one single skill from us that will last us our whole life. We need to master a variety of skills as our life progresses. We have to be like a carpenter with an array of tools that we choose from depending on our circumstances. We need to know precisely when to use a chisel and when to use a plane, when we need a saw and when we need a hammer. As this analogy illustrates, even if we possess a range of skills, we need to decide when and where to use what. It is only when we master this ability that we become useful and beneficial to the place where we belong.

To use the right skills in the right circumstances, we need to sharpen our skills and know exactly which ones are useful in which kinds of situations. Otherwise, we are unable to use our skills to their full potential. If we try to use a six-inch nail to join together two pieces of wood that are only one inch thick, it will not work, because the nail will protrude out the opposite side. Nails can be very useful for joining pieces of wood, but if we don't use the right kind of nail, it could end up damaging the wood. This is an obvious example, but many readers may find it difficult to accept when it comes to their own circumstances. In fact, those who are not happy with how they are treated often believe that it is very unfair that they don't get promoted or recognized by their bosses when they are so capable in their job. What they may not realize is that we work not to prove our capability, but to create profits and benefits for many people in society. That's how we can increase the value of our work. The company or organization we work for is not like a school where we receive grades or certification based on our performance.

The more capable we are, the harder we need to work to transform our ability into usefulness. Highly educated people are often confident in their ability and feel that they are superior to others. And their self-confidence helps them do high-quality work. But no matter how superior their academic achievement is, they will not make use of their ability unless they are put in a position where they can utilize it. Many people mistakenly believe that their academic background is proof of their capability. They often cannot accept the results they are confronted with, so they instead blame their colleagues or working environment for not recognizing and bringing out their full potential.

What we need to do is to shift from being a capable person to being a beneficial person. It doesn't matter if you haven't yet been able to use all your skills. There is always a proper order for everything. If we want to build a house, we need to first cut down timber in the woods. Then we need to plane pillars before creating the framework and having the roof tiled. We cannot skip any steps to reach the next stage.

Look within, and contemplate whether you are being beneficial to the place you belong to or are simply trying to prove your capability. This will help you fulfill the second condition for career advancement.

～ 4 ～

THE THIRD CONDITION
FOR A SUCCESSFUL CAREER
USE OTHER PEOPLE'S SKILLS

To succeed in your career, you must lead the people who follow you. The more successful you become, the more people you will look after. The number of people you guide should increase year by year as you climb the ladder of success. This means that your workload overflows, which naturally leads you to use others' assistance to do what you cannot do yourself. Let's say you have five people working for you right now. As you get promoted, the number of people you rely on may increase to twenty and eventually, when you become an executive officer, to a hundred.

The ability to achieve as an individual is different from the ability to help your team succeed. If you consider how many people may be working under you as you become successful, you will be able to start cultivating the ability to make good use of other people's assistance.

No matter how talented a person may be as an individual, he will not be able to maintain his success unless he can get work done through others. A sales representative may be able to achieve amazing results when working on her own, but she may not be able to help her assistants bring in the additional sales that the team needs. We may be able to prove how skillful we are in the work we do on our own, but we may not be skillful at using the skills of other people.

For example, we may have exceptional DIY skills, but that doesn't mean that we'd be able to construct a large building on our own. The skills required to construct a skyscraper are different from the skills required to build a kennel or fix a roof. If we set out to build a skyscraper, we will need a team of professionals who can draw up blueprints, plan and raise funds, and hire and direct construction workers. Completing a big project like that requires the ability to lead and instruct others.

As you've probably guessed by now, the third condition for climbing the ladder of success is to know when to use our own ability and when to use others' ability as we work to achieve our goals. And as we progress, we need to shift the balance from using our own skills to using other people's skills.

We all know that Napoleon Bonaparte was a great general, but even he would have been defeated if he had had to fight against one hundred soldiers, or perhaps even just ten soldiers, all by himself. His personal ability would have only allowed him to defeat one, two, or three soldiers at most, but he became an undefeated general when he led an army of hundreds of thousands.

Understanding this difference in ability is crucial for career advancement. But people who do not see the difference or would rather focus on improving their individual skills can pursue the path of a specialist. We are all born with different talents and preferences, so there is nothing wrong with focusing in one area. But cultivating our individual, specialized skills is usually not sufficient to advance in a career. We certainly have to rely on our own ability at the start of our career. But as we accumulate knowledge and skills, we need to gradually shift our focus to using the skills and winning the hearts of other people. In other words, we need management skills.

The basis of managerial skill is the ability to discern other people's capabilities. This ability enables us to see other people's strengths and weaknesses. Managerial ability also means knowing how best to maximize other people's potential and place them in the right places based on their abilities. The essential skill required of the manager is to see and assess other people's innate qualities and characteristics—even those that they themselves are not aware of.

~ 5 ~
THREE WAYS TO UNDERSTAND
HUMAN BEINGS MORE DEEPLY

Learning about and understanding human beings—how we think, act, live, and relate with one another—is a crucial element in mastering the third condition for a successful career. There are three basic ways to do this. First, we can learn from our own experiences. We can learn lessons and gain insight about people through our interactions with others. The second way is to find someone we respect to follow as a teacher and learn from that person how to cultivate accurate insights and develop acute observation skills and keen perceptive abilities. This allows us to gain the wisdom necessary to accurately assess people and events.

The third way to learn about human beings may sound obvious: it is to read many books. I would like to mention four kinds of books that are more useful than others. First, biographies of great historical figures contain stories about how they made a name for themselves, so a good biography can be a bible of success. A second genre to read is history, because knowing the past helps us foresee the future. Studying various historical events, how historical figures coped with them, and the outcomes of their actions enables us to foresee the problems that are likely to arise in the circumstance we will face in the future. This process can be identical to how we prepare for exams. We study past exam questions to predict the actual exam questions that we will need to solve.

The third type of book to read is literature and poetry, which teaches us what touches people's hearts. Different things motivate different people. Some are motivated to take action by intellect, others by reason. But I think the strongest incentive is emotion. To motivate many people to take action, we have to engage them emotionally. Developing an interest in literature and art is a vital step toward understanding the feelings of others. Reading literature and poetry allows us to discover what moves people, inspires them, and touches their hearts.

Fourth and last, but by no means least, we do well to read books of religious and spiritual teachings. In terms of importance, religious and spiritual books should be placed at the top of the list, since they move people at an even deeper level than literature does. These books convey the Will of God, so reading them helps us develop an unshakable core at the depths of our heart. This unshakable mind becomes the power to overcome the trials and difficulties we face in life. Climbing the ladder of success and becoming a leader requires continuous effort to deepen our understanding and master the workings of people's hearts and minds.

To sum up, the three conditions for climbing the ladder of success are as follows: The first condition is to find joy in working. We need to work hard and love working. The second condition is to become a useful and beneficial person instead of just a capable person. The third condition is to analyze our work and discern what we can do on our own and what is beyond our capability. If we feel that the task is too much to handle on our own, we should use other people's skills. To do so requires management skills, which we can cultivate by studying a wide range of subjects.

These three conditions apply to all kinds of jobs and situations. It is my sincere wish that you will take to heart these universal conditions for success and use them as guidelines as you continue your diligent efforts to walk the path to success.

CHAPTER 4

ADVANCING *with the* HEART *of* LEADERSHIP

~ 1 ~
TRUE LEADERS
FACE ADVERSITY SELFLESSLY

Many of us want to achieve more than just
making headway in our careers. We also
aspire to be leaders at what we do. So what can we do
to fulfill this aspiration? Leadership demands more
from us than advancing our career. Since we are spiritual beings, we should aim to rise to leadership and
grow spiritually at the same time, so we can become
the kind of leader who can produce limitless happiness. To be this kind of leader, we need a selfless
heart. My definition of a true leader is someone who
meets this higher standard of spiritual character. If
we ever ignore our spiritual responsibility and abuse
our authority, our leadership will only bring suffering to many people. Such a leader is headed toward
spiritual decline and will not be able to fulfill the
duties of true leadership.

Today, many global issues are challenging the world's leaders. We think of our world leaders as the best in the world at what they do, but they will prove their real leadership ability by how well they handle adversity. True leadership is difficult to identify in rosy circumstances, because there is nothing challenging about using power and making decisions when things are going well. But there are big differences in how people lead in times of adversity, and in these situations, true leaders shine. While many people become frantic and think mostly about protecting themselves when they face tough problems, true leaders stay composed. They do not suddenly turn fierce and begin oppressing people whom they fear could be out to strip them of their power. No matter how misunderstood true leaders are, they carry on calmly through difficult times. While they wait for circumstances to improve, they continue to develop themselves so they will be prepared when the next opportunity to show their abilities comes along.

My philosophy of leadership applies to business leaders as much as political leaders. For example, if an employee's work brings growth to the company partially thanks to favorable trends in the industry, she may advance far in the company. But whether this advancement was truly deserved and whether she has the makings of a real leader will be tested in the future, at some point during the thirty to forty years of her career, when she faces challenging circumstances. She will be challenged by her weaknesses, which will appear when the winds of good fortune slow down, come to a halt, or turn against her.

In the unstable economic and international conditions we face today, we need much more in our leaders than a history of personal success. The people of a country or an organization need the leadership of men and women who have taken on adversity despite disadvantages to themselves. We need leaders who have tested their abilities through unfavorable circumstances, have willingly taken on undesirable work, or have worked diligently to succeed in obscure industries. These are the men and women who will be the real leaders of our future.

Many of the businesses that have achieved significant growth in recent years have benefited from a booming economy, but the economic boom will soon end, and the economy will face many crises. When these tough times come, the captain of the ship must know how to handle crisis. He will need nerves of steel and physical vigor, which can only be honed through experience, to help him persevere through the ordeal.

My message to everyone, especially today's youth, is to stop looking for experience in popular work and go after undesirable jobs instead. We shouldn't determine who has leadership potential based solely on the reputation of the colleges we went to or the companies we work for. Willingly expose yourself to adverse circumstances. Be ambitious enough to bet your future on a career that is still obscure. Challenge and ambition are what dreams are made of. Many people dream of graduating from a prestigious university, working for a major corporation, and becoming an executive. Even though these achievements may make you a leader by today's standards, you should aspire to do much more than spend your life working on an equation that someone already solved. There is nothing exciting about solving an easy equation. Achieving success is far more rewarding when it demands a lot of hard work.

2

THE BEST AND BRIGHTEST ARE SEEKING DIFFERENT KINDS OF INDUSTRIES

Allowing our success to be determined by the college we attended or the company we are working for can lead to hardships down the road. We can already see examples of these kinds of hardships. Many decades ago, the top graduates from the best Japanese universities were employed by steel companies and a privatized Japan National Railways. This was a time when steel manufacturing and rail was still the backbone of the nation and was a prestigious industry to work for. But steel no longer has the prestige it once had.

The civil service industry has gone through the same kind of decline over the years. Until the latter part of the twentieth century, civil service jobs were considered important positions of high status. Ambitious graduates of elite universities used to dream of filling these posts. But today, these positions are low-prestige, and civil service careers are in decline.

This reversal has occurred because many people are suffering under the burden of big government. The communist systems of developed countries are falling apart because this system made the mistake of promoting a bloated government that had to be supported by oppressed citizens. If a government employs too many people in regulatory jobs, the nation spends too much of its energy inhibiting the activity and suppressing the vigor of the people, and when that happens, decline is inevitable. By contrast, a good government is one that is small and fosters national wealth and development by invigorating the growth and prosperity of the people. A good government trusts the confidence and courage of its people and their booming enterprises. With this type of government, the entire country is able to flourish as it should.

In the coming years, people will face the choice between a big government and a small government. The people of the world will want enough freedom to create prosperity for themselves and for their country. As international trends are strongly hinting, I predict that a small government will be the most popular choice. If this prediction comes true, what has happened in civil service will happen in other industries: jobs that were once sought after by the best and brightest will face a crisis. The most talented people will start to seek jobs that are undesirable and avoided by most people, and these careers will start to become popular. For example, industries such as information technology, which deals with products and services that cannot be directly seen or touched, and fashion, which requires good taste and an imagination, will rise into popularity.

3

AIM FOR NEW FRONTIERS

These days, companies are emerging and disappearing so quickly that they only last an average of thirty years. As all these changes suggest, jobs and industries will change rapidly over the course of a career. This means that if you aspire to be a leader, you must seek a future in industries that have just sprouted and are not yet fully developed and prosperous. New leaders will come from undeveloped industries, where they will have an opportunity to test themselves, ride out uncertainty, and develop the ability to show people the way forward. For example, people with academic degrees will bet their future on careers that have little to do with their field of study. Degrees and certifications are a big trend, but in the near future, many people will willingly disregard their degrees and certifications in pursuit of new frontiers.

For example, medicine has been such a highly valued profession that a huge number of outstanding students have chosen to go to medical school. But many people have been drawn to medicine not because they feel a true calling but because medicine offers the same high status and large incomes that we find in the corporate world. Popular professions inevitably attract many people without aptitude. Soon there will be a large surplus of doctors, and many of them will reconsider their vocation and decide to change careers. There will be doctors who decide to disregard their medical degree and pursue a completely different type of job. Engineers and scientists with master's and doctoral degrees will challenge themselves in completely different genres. The future will be full of people who willingly choose the more challenging path of pursuing a new career.

In the near future, outstanding people will choose between two career directions. The first career option will be small venture businesses or startups that are not yet well-known but are suited to their academic history, skill sets, and experiences and will put their abilities to the test. The second career option will be to pursue a completely different genre from what they studied in school. For example, we may have economists who started out with a degree in law, engineers who have a degree in literature, and entrepreneurs with a degree in medicine. These two career directions will become increasingly important as it becomes harder to learn about the future in university courses and specialized programs. These programs are mostly outdated by the time they are taught to students.

Hints for creating the coming age and clues to opening a path to the future can be found right now, in the real world, and in the approaching waves of the future. We have to keep our senses sharpened and on high alert to sniff out and ride these trends as soon as they come. From now on, we will be able to earn a living in careers that are not necessarily based on what we studied in school. More specifically, new leaders will be working with the heart and mind. Their work may or may not be a religious vocation. But at the least, these leaders will find their life purpose in working for the happiness of people's hearts.

Some of the best and brightest now are pursuing careers in the financial sector and in information technology, which are gaining popularity and earning high incomes. But these people will soon begin to search for a purposeful life beyond playing the money game and exchanging information for profit. They will begin to look for their calling in the age-old but ever evolving study of the human heart and mind.

～ 4 ～
LEADERS WORK FOR HAPPINESS
FROM THEIR HEARTS

I cannot stress enough that new leaders will dedicate their lives to the happiness of the human heart. This trend is, in a way, a reaction to the problems of our current economy. Many people who have struggled their way through the competitive world of business will start to seek a return to a pure and healthy state of mind.

Careers that work with matters of the heart and mind will eventually become big and profitable. Just as steel was once the backbone of the country, the human heart will be the new backbone of the country and the world. Not only will new careers emerge from this vocation, but this new work will also create opportunities for part-time jobs and side businesses, because everyone will have increasingly more spare time in the future. New leaders will show that everyone was born to fulfill a purpose besides the jobs we hold to earn a living, and they'll be able to recommend ways we can use our free time to pursue higher values. For example, the current trend in obtaining certifications for professional skills will eventually be replaced by a new trend of becoming teachers of the mind.

5

THE THREE CONDITIONS
OF LEADERSHIP

N ew leaders will fulfill a different set of conditions from commonly accepted standards.
There will be three new conditions. The first condition is for our leaders to demonstrate outstanding
achievement during the first twenty years or the first
half of their lives. Even though many leaders will be
pursuing careers that are not related to their field
of study, it is still important that they gain skills in
some kind of discipline, for example, medicine, law,
engineering, or any other field—even something like
professional sports. Showing an aptitude for outstanding ability and excellence will be the first condition for being recognized by society as a leader.

The second condition for being recognized as
a leader is having had experience riding out a huge
crisis, suffering, facing adversity, or fearlessly relin-

quishing your credentials in pursuit of a new frontier in spite of the hardships. Willingly putting oneself through challenges and unfavorable circumstances, despite having had the choice of an easier path, will bring well-earned praise and respect from many people.

The third condition is having the ability to create something new by fusing past experience with the new career. Let's say that a doctor decides to pursue a new career in business management. Everything about this business will be new to him and may need some getting used to in the beginning. But when his new abilities develop enough and his career starts to take off, where will he focus his attention? Most managers are focused on making profits, and most of their attention is directed at the bottom line. But a manager with prior experience in medical practice may come up with a completely different mission for his company. He may think of ways that the company will be able to contribute to bettering the health of society or come up with ideas for improving the health and productivity of his employees.

Each of these three conditions is a dialectic stage that results in the production of higher-value work through the synthesis of two opposing qualities. In the first stage, we see the thesis; in the second, the antithesis; and the third stage brings the synthesis. In the doctor-turned-business-manager's case, what he produces will be a business with a mission in medicine. By repeatedly working through the three conditions, we will produce new ideas.

Let's look at another example. Let's say that someone with a degree in engineering or the sciences pursues a new career in the financial sector, where workers commonly have degrees in business, economics, or law. Once the engineer gets the hang of things and makes some headway in her company, she may come up with new formulas that produce more accurate financial calculations, or she may create a new, science-based, financial projection method that could revolutionize the entire industry. Or, if a law school graduate decides to become a novelist because she wants to write stories about how the real world works, she may be able to write not just about people's hearts but also realistic depictions of how her characters' lives are affected by society. This will give her novels a unique twist unlike the stories produced by other writers. So, there will be a new trend in the future toward thinking differently to produce new things. This will become a wonderful social advancement that everyone will appreciate.

In conclusion, the first condition of new leadership is to be recognized as talented at an early stage in life. The second condition is to use that talent to succeed in the face of unfavorable circumstances. And the final condition is to take that success a step further by applying past experiences to produce something completely new. Being able to fulfill these three conditions is vital to navigating through uncharted waters, and the experiences gained from them will earn people's recognition. The effort we give to these conditions not only nurtures our leadership in the real world, but also nurtures our spiritual growth by enabling us to widen the horizons of our souls and reach new heights.

CHAPTER 5

WORKING *with* *a* SPIRIT *of* LOVE

1

HOW IS WORK RELATED TO LOVE?

In this day and age, work is a huge part of daily life, and we gain a better perspective on work when we consider its relationship to spiritual Truths. So in this chapter, I would like to discuss how to think about work and handle our job in accordance with God's Truths.

To begin with, what place does work have among the teachings of the Truths? Those studying Buddhism may say that work is about Right Action—a part of the Eightfold Path. Theoretically speaking, it is true that Right Action is about doing one's job properly. But the principle of Right Action only helps us review our work from an introspective perspective, and that isn't sufficient to grasp the overall picture of work. To accurately perceive the place of work in life, we need to take a more proactive approach.

The proactive approach I offer is based on the relationship between the essence of work and a spirit of love. I wonder if anyone has ever seriously considered this topic. I don't think many people have thought deeply about how devotion to work might be closely connected to the principle of love. Those who have considered this topic may understand that love involves thinking about others and serving the common good. Work, then, serves as a catalyst of love because it is one way that we can contribute to society. I am, of course, in complete agreement with this view; I believe that the ultimate goal of our work is to help create an ideal world on earth. But I wish to further expand on the relationship between work and love by considering the personal, private roles that work plays in our lives.

I have been examining the nature of love from various angles for some time, and I have shared my thoughts on this topic on many occasions. For example, I have said that the essence of love lies in giving unconditionally, without seeking anything in return.

I have said, too, that love is being kind to others but that its expression sometimes can be stern or strong. These aspects of love—kindness, sternness, and strength—are all indispensable facets of love that we need to take into account in our consideration of the relationship between love and work.

Kindness, or being nice to others, helps us develop smooth relationships and serves as a powerful force that drives and facilitates our work. When we want to nurture others, our love may sometimes appear harsh. This sternness can help the people we love grow and cultivate their skills so they can perform at a higher level. Love can also be our strength—for example, love can lead us to feel responsible for our job or protect the people working under us. Love's strength can also manifest as the enthusiasm to develop our business.

Another aspect of love is attentiveness. You can see this dimension of love in the way a mother cradles and takes care of her newborn baby. The mother thinks hard about why her baby is crying and gives attentive care—checking the diaper and providing food—to make sure the baby is comfortable. Love embodies this sort of attentiveness, not only when a mother cares for her baby, but also when a worker does a perfect, flawless job. Attentiveness, judiciousness, and keen awareness of other people's needs are all aspects of love.

2
EMPATHY:
THE KEY TO WORKING WITH LOVE

Although some people work on their own, most of us work with others—our colleagues, bosses, subordinates, and clients. This interaction enables us to do our job and makes our work more meaningful.

Work resembles love in this sense. Love exists between people; it connects us and creates relationships between us. In the same way, work creates relationships between people. For example, paperwork serves as a means of communication among people. Business documents are a form of public correspondence that not only convey our thoughts to others, but also provide the information they need. Whether we are preparing these documents for our bosses or our clients, we need to place ourselves in their situation and see things from their perspective. There are always others who need the document that we are creating, and if it is full of mistakes, then we are wasting their time. Slapdash work overloads others with extra work and steals their valuable time. In this sense, doing sloppy work is taking love from others.

Someone who always makes mistakes and errors at work is like a child who wants to be the center of attention all the time. Others will have to constantly check everything he does. From a spiritual perspective, such a person is actually taking love from others, because others have to spend extra time and energy taking care of him.

The idea of doing a perfect, flawless work may sound a bit severe. All of us have made mistakes at some point in life, and we know how bad they make us feel. We've all blamed ourselves for the mistakes we have made, and remorse may linger in our hearts to this day. Many of us fret over the feeling that we are incompetent, careless, or flawed.

But when we think of work as a manifestation of love, we see how the spiritual laws of love apply to the work we do. What we need to practice at work is empathy and putting ourselves in others' shoes. We need to consider the people for whom we are doing our job and make sure that we are providing what they need. This is the most important aspect of work.

3
WORK IS ABOUT
SERVING PEOPLE'S NEEDS

There are basically two types of people who can't do their jobs successfully. The first type includes those who lack the ability to do what their position requires of them. The second type includes those who possess exceptional abilities that actually prevent them from cooperating with others or working as part of a team. In an organization, both of these types of people often cause trouble for other people.

Immersing ourselves in the pursuit of perfection sometimes causes trouble for others, because the pursuit of perfection can devolve into a preoccupation with ourselves. If we are only concerned about doing work that satisfies ourselves, then we are just using work to try to prove our ability. This attitude is spiritually immature. As we progress in our career, we realize that it is simply unacceptable to only do what satisfies us, what makes sense to us, or what makes us feel better.

You may wish to do a perfect job, but you need to consider how other people feel about it, and you may sometimes need to go with what they want. People who have to do everything their way eventually find themselves shunned by the people they work with. This is one reason why some intelligent people cannot get ahead at work. Good grades at university do not guarantee success in the real world. Even those with praiseworthy academic achievements may end up doing menial work. These are often the type of scholarly people who only pursue work that they feel is worth doing and do not see the needs of their company, department, or section. These people often get caught up in fulfilling their complacent appetite for knowledge or following familiar procedures and do not see how important it is to keep an overall balance. No matter how smart they are, if they cannot cooperate, they will gradually alienate others and will be unlikely to take an important position in the organization. This is the harsh reality that awaits this type of person.

Work is a manifestation of love, so we should look at our work from a perspective higher than our own and strive to create the best results for everyone. While some people, such as artists, have occupations that require them to pursue originality, for most of us, success depends on meeting the needs of a large number of people. A quick and accurate understanding of the demands and wants of the people is indispensable to success in most jobs.

Another important element of success is a swift understanding of the expectations of your boss. Does your boss prefer that you to do an accurate job, paying careful attention to detail? Or does she prefer that you work quickly? First and foremost, you need to grasp exactly what your boss expects of you.

If we want to do work that benefits the world, we must pay attention to the needs and demands of the people. Society functions when each of us works to supply what others need, and that's how the majority of people earn their living. It is this mutual need that makes a society into a community. So to succeed at our work, we must thoroughly meet other people's demands.

✦ 4 ✦
SERVICE-MINDEDNESS
IS PART OF THE SPIRIT OF LOVE

Meeting other people's needs is the same as providing good service. Some people may take the phrase *good service* to mean something superficial, frivolous, or even money-driven. But I believe that it is the spirit of love that makes us want to provide good service to others.

Our heartfelt desire to satisfy the wishes of others is something that we should be proud of. A wish to provide something that can improve people's lives and to be a part of fulfilling the needs of the maximum number of people—this is the kind of mindset we need to have at work.

There are many aspects to the work you do, but one thing is clear. If your work is inconveniencing others, then, from a spiritual perspective, you are actually taking love from them. Remember, you are giving love when you can bring joy to many people through your work.

It's also important to consider whether you are the right person for the job. Look within yourself carefully, and consider why you want that job in the first place. You may find that you only want it because it will bring you higher status or a higher position. If you have the abilities necessary to fulfill the tasks that important position requires of you, you will be able to offer love to a lot of people. But if you are not competent, you may end up taking love from a lot of people.

If the whole purpose of your success is to gain respect in society rather than to serve others, your career advancement could have a negative impact. Think of your success as a gift from God, and focus on the work through which you can make the most of your strengths and redeem your shortcomings. This is the true spirit of work.

Service-mindedness is a great force that infuses your work with the energy of love. Attending to other people's needs, devoting your heart to your work, working sincerely and honestly—these are all essential to doing good work. If you wish to be a giver of love, start by putting your heart into your everyday work, and heartily fulfill other people's needs. You will find that everything, including your life and the lives of people around you, will begin to move in a positive direction.

CHAPTER 6

UNLEASHING *the* POWER *of* REST

⌒ 1 ⌒
RELAXATION IS ESSENTIAL
TO HAPPINESS

Persistent effort, perseverance, and the pursuit of self-growth are essential to living a good life, and, for that reason, they are a consistent theme in my books. But there is much more to happiness than working hard and aiming higher. Happiness also lies in the simple things in life that bring us delight, such as the bliss we find in relaxation. This is a timeless Truth that has been cherished by everyone throughout the ages. If you are feeling stuck in your work, my philosophy and method of working will help you find balance between active and quiet happiness and enable you to conquer your obstacles.

Schools and companies provide summer vacations, for example, because they are restorative to our body and mind. Rest relieves fatigue and replenishes vitality so we can return to our work completely rejuvenated. I am sure that the industriousness of the Japanese people, who are known for taking few breaks and working long hours, has contributed to Japan's remarkable growth and prosperity. But I am also fascinated by the philosophy of work in western cultures, where I personally have had career experience. To use an analogy, workaholics in Japan remind me of hardworking ants and bees, who are constantly flying or marching around to forage for pollen and food.

Western cultures think of work differently. Workers in western cultures remind me of lions. The lion focuses its energy on do-or-die situations, such as hunting prey. In these situations, failure is not an option, so the lion is 100 percent determined to succeed. When it dashes for its prey, it moves with speed and agility. By expending every ounce of muscle on a single precision attack, the lion unleashes such extraordinary power that the zebra never stands a chance. But after the beast has released all this destructive force and satisfied its hunger, it stops working to find prey. All that is left to do is to take a well-deserved nap under the savanna sun or beneath the cool shade of a tree.

2

FIND BALANCE
BETWEEN WORK AND REST

T he lion's way of life reminds me of the coil spring. For a coil spring to bounce high, it also needs to be good at contracting. Being always stretched out or constantly compressed weakens the coil and can make it stop working the way it should. The best coils are the ones that contract well, because they are capable of bouncing very high and then quickly contracting again. This alternating pattern between bouncing high and compressing down is a lot like the lion's life.

The bees and ants that are used to sweating and working every day may criticize the lion for wasting time and being slow and lazy. What they don't realize is that once the lion gets to work, it is capable of a fury of activity beyond the imagination of any bee or ant. I don't mean to generalize these working styles to everyone, but I find that people who have accomplished great things often live by the lion's way of life.

Everyone's life has seasons of accomplishment. Growth never progresses in a stick-straight line upward, because our abilities naturally develop in stages. When our abilities reach a certain stage, our development flattens out into a period of sluggish progress. But eventually, a time will suddenly come when an explosive surge of reserved potential bursts forth. We'll realize that we've suddenly come remarkably far in our growth. We alternate between these two stages throughout life. If you look back on your life, you will see that this fluctuating cycle has been a part of your growth, too.

Some occasions call for a burst of decisive action. They require the power to dash up the cliff that blocks our way forward. And then, when the cliff is cleared, we will have a chance to relax. There will be a large stretch of flat grassland that we can stroll through with ease. Eventually, we will encounter yet another steep cliff, and that cliff will be followed by another level plateau.

We can think of life as a journey through many repetitions of this cycle. Life does not confront us with adversity all the time. Adversity happens perhaps a few times, at most, in the course of a year. So when our path is smooth, it's vital to reserve our strength, like the coil, so that when adversity comes, we'll be able to give it all our strength and intelligence. This philosophy of work is common in western cultures, but it is not a well-understood way of thinking among the Japanese. When Japanese people see someone who takes a break one minute and works furiously the next, they tend to see that person as lazy and capricious. A complete disengagement from work or study would justify criticism, but breaks are not always unproductive; there are positive ways of taking a break that guarantee improvement in productivity.

❦ 3 ❦
REST KEEPS US
IN OUR BEST CONDITION

During the latter half of the twentieth century, the industriousness of the Japanese people captured the world's attention, and Japan's prosperity inspired the envy of many nations. In times like these, when the whole world's attention is upon us, we need grander visions and endeavors of greater value. Although the diligence of an ant or a bee is essential, occasions like this call for people who can work like the lion. I recommend the industrious life to most people. But I hope that many of the people who have opened their minds to the spiritual Truths I offer will choose to live more often like the lion.

If you are reading this book, chances are that you have great potential hidden within you. My readers are not only very intelligent and wonderful people, but also good, kind, tremendously loving, and naturally faithful believers. Once their zeal is ignited, they will act with the fury of a lion, and the whole prairie will rise into flames. You have tremendous power and agility with you. Because you have this potential, it is important to shift your concept of work so that you can draw that power out of yourself when you need it.

When you start to take on bigger work, think about why the lion is capable of such explosive strength. Lions can suddenly burst into a sprint because they are using the energy they have saved to activate every fiber in their muscles toward a goal that really counts. To be capable of expending so much physical power, they work to bring themselves up to tiptop condition. Otherwise, it would be impossible for them to perform at their very best.

People who steadily use up their energy, little by little, tend to become exhausted and are never in their best working condition. If you find yourself doing this, you will benefit from changing the way you think about your working style. Rather than wasting a lot of valuable energy indiscriminately, find the one goal that requires the most time and attention. When you have decided which goal to focus on, start doing whatever it takes to bring yourself into your absolute best condition so that you can give this goal everything you've got.

4
REGULAR REST BOOSTS PRODUCTIVITY

Taking breaks conscientiously is essential for keeping yourself in good condition. Doing this will especially help industrious people make more productive use of their days off. Giving yourself time to rest and rejuvenate is a truly indispensable life practice.

There is an economic principle called the law of diminishing returns, also known as the principle of diminishing marginal productivity. According to this principle, the satisfaction we gain from any endeavor decreases with every additional unit of measure we invest in it. For example, if you are extremely hungry for several hours, the first piece of toast you eat will be exquisitely delicious. The second piece of toast may still be delicious, but not as much as the first. Your toast will get less and less appetizing the more you eat, until you have finally had so much that you don't want any more. The level of satisfaction that your toast brings you will probably be down to zero by your fifth slice.

The same principle is at work when we study. During our student years, we all had days when we had to study all day for an exam. Anyone in this situation is challenged by the fact that we absorb less and less information as the day progresses. We are able to cover a lot in the first hour, but our concentration diminishes considerably by the second or third hour. Our mind starts to wander, our attention becomes scattered, and we can't remember as much as we could when we first started studying. Some of us who emphasize the importance of willpower would keep going anyway, studying for five hours or even as many as twelve hours, even after noticing that we are no longer absorbing much. Based on my experience, however, productivity increases substantially when we take ten-minute breaks after every hour of study, instead of spending three straight hours trying to study uninterruptedly. This may sound simple, but it is a time-tested principle.

This brings us back to the main theme of this chapter. Developing the habit of taking regular breaks is vital to increasing your productivity. I even recommend this habit for your daily spiritual practice. If you spend all day, every day, studying spiritual books, the law of diminishing returns will start to take effect. This way of studying fills your spiritual appetite beyond the brim, eventually leaving no room for any more. So if you ever find yourself in this situation, take a break from your studies for a little while, and look for a more efficient method of studying.

For example, if you designate Sundays for studying, take breaks throughout the day rather than spending the entire day with your face buried in your books. If you routinely study every day, you might consider a new routine of studying five days a week and spending two days away from your books. Of course, you want to choose what works best for you. You could even go with six days of study and one day of rest.

You can also schedule your study routine on a monthly basis. You could designate three weeks for studying and one week for a break. Or you could reserve two out of three months for studying and one whole month for a long vacation. There are any number of ways you can plan your schedule. The key is to remember that taking breaks is not laziness. It is an important part of improving the productivity of your work life. This is the positive effect that makes rest indispensable to our lives.

5

REST AND VARIETY PRODUCE PERFORMANCE

What if we have been working on a subject for so long that we have become bored and our productivity has noticeably diminished, but there is just not enough time to take a break? What can we do? If a break is out of the question, changing the subject can be almost as effective. Alternating among a variety of subjects keeps things interesting enough to help us concentrate longer. For example, we could pick up a different book to read. We could also alternate between the three senses, from reading to writing to listening.

Varying your location is another way of mixing things up to keep things interesting. Your home office can be your reading spot, your bedroom can be where you listen to audiobooks, and the living room can be the place you review your notes. These are some of the ways I give myself a change of pace to refresh my mind and make more efficient and fruitful use of my time. The key is to find creative ways to make the most of the limited hours we have each day.

If you ever do so much reading that you get tired of books, try avoiding reading for an entire week. At the end of the week, you will find yourself settling down to it again with a fresh mind. Not reading for an entire week may feel like laziness, but it really isn't.

I cannot stress enough that we should not feel wrong for including regular breaks in our work routine. This is a style of work that is vital to improving our productivity. So if you find your productivity and performance diminishing, change what you are working on and change where you are working. Keeping things varied will lift your spirits. Then, incorporate actual rest into your routine and wait until you feel revived. Variety and rest will keep you physically, mentally, and intellectually rejuvenated. This is a method of working that is vital for accomplishing big things in life.

CHAPTER 7

MAKING
the MOST *of*
the GIFT *of* TIME

~ 1 ~

TIME IS A PRECIOUS GIFT

Our happiness or unhappiness is determined not only by the outcome of the events we face, but also by the quality of the time we spend as we live in this world. When we look back at our life, we can review either the events we've experienced or the way we've used our time. Time is a vital measure of our life, and raising the average quality of the time we spend will enhance the overall quality of our life.

First, let us ponder the nature of time. Needless to say, one day is made up of twenty-four hours. This is an immutable fact. It is such an invaluable and strict law of life that no politician, king, or philosopher can change it. No one—not even Einstein, who developed the theory of relativity—can extend or shorten those twenty-four hours by a single second. Even as I write this, the seconds are ticking away ephemerally, like sand slipping and falling through our fingers. It seems as if the time we have spent is lost forever.

We cannot escape the fact that every one of a day's twenty-four hours is made up of sixty minutes and that every minute is made up of sixty seconds. Every human activity occurs within time, and time has been an indispensable element in bearing the fruit of civilizations and achieving the feats of human history.

In the ocean, waves constantly surge upon and withdraw from the shore. Waves exist solely because of this continual movement of pushing and pulling. But we human beings are different. We are here to achieve something within the continuous flow of time. It's regrettable that many people squander their time without ever considering how it can be used to benefit and empower their lives.

I would like to ask my readers to become aware of the true value of time once again. Time is truly precious, and it is something that no one can take away from you. No matter what circumstances you are in or what you do, no one can deprive you of the twenty-four hours that each day gives you. This time is a treasure given only to you, as precious as gold or diamonds, and its value will stay with you forever. Time is indeed the greatest gift of God and a sign of His compassion.

Jesus Christ and all the other great figures in history had the same twenty-four hours a day to achieve their accomplishments. But the last three years of Jesus's life were probably more intense than anyone else's thirty-six months. We are all given the same twenty-four hours a day, but it's up to each one of us to put our time to great use. That's why it's important for us to earnestly consider how to make the best use of the time given to us and how to create as much value as we can from it.

2
WHERE DO WE WASTE OUR TIME?

Time passes like the sand in an hourglass. Each second is as precious as pure gold, so time elapsing is like gold dust constantly falling away and disappearing. How are you spending this precious time every day? What do you do with the time at your disposal? Where do you waste your time?

Anyone who claims to have never wasted a single second of the day is either truly exceptional, lying, or not seeing things clearly. So if we want to make the most of our time, we have to begin by thinking about how not to waste it. Seeing time as as valuable as gold helps us keep from using our time carelessly. Instead of letting it simply fall away, we should concentrate on how we can make every grain of gold sparkle.

Let me share with you what my personal experience has taught me about making the best use of our time. When you look back and review how you spent your day, where do you think you wasted the most time? Some may say they wasted time sleeping, and others may say eating or taking a bath. But the time we spend eating, sleeping, and otherwise sustaining our life is not a waste. These things are a necessary part of life, and ignoring our physiological needs results in severe consequences. Where we actually waste the most time is in our work or studies. This is the conclusion I have come to after many years of careful thought. We waste time not in things that we consider futile, but in what we believe to be beneficial. We are much more apt to waste our time doing what we believe to be valuable.

This may sound quite paradoxical, but if you imagine yourself in your twilight years, nearing the end of your life, you'll know how true these words are. What do you think you'll regret at the end of your life? Will you regret spending time sleeping or eating? Do you think you'll regret spending your leisure time swimming or playing tennis or golf? I don't think so. You'll probably wish you could have done more in your work or studies. Your regret will most likely be not having been able to accomplish what you wanted in the job or studies in which you spent most of your life.

~~~ 3 ~~~
Applying the 80-20 Rule to Life

You've probably heard of the Pareto Principle, also known as the 80-20 rule, which states that, in anything we do, 80 percent of the results come from the 20 percent of the causes. Let's say that a company makes a profit of one million dollars. Based on this principle, 20 percent of the employees make eight hundred thousand dollars, or 80 percent of the company's income. Similarly, if the company's revenue were ten billion dollars, eight billion would have been earned by 20 percent of the staff.

The Pareto Principle can be applied to any work setting, organization, or group of people. In any area of life, twenty percent plays an essential role. In other words, managing the 20 percent allows us to take charge of 80 percent of the whole.

For instance, if you work for ten hours a day, you

achieve most of your day's work within two hours. These two hours are the only time that brings you substantial results and leads you to make great accomplishments. What you do during that 20 percent of your working day determines your success for the day, while your work during the remaining 80 percent of the day does not produce much result.

In personnel management, too, it is difficult to manage everybody working in a large corporation. But if you can hold a firm grip on the 20 percent in the key positions, you will be able to manage the other 80 percent, or the majority of the staff.

The same holds true for retail businesses. Business owners make various forecasts and analyses, but the critical factor for success boils down to 20 percent of what they do. One-fifth of their entire business determines the whole company's future. It's about emphasizing or accentuating some parts over others. Instead of going about your daily duties without any concrete plan or making analyses without a specific goal, try grasping the most important 20 percent. That will allow you to concentrate on the most crucial part and lead you to accomplishment and success.

A common reason we sometimes fail in life is our perfectionism. The drawback of this desire to be perfect is that if we never accept anything less than 100 percent, we may end up with nothing. It is like a baseball player who aims for a home run at every bat but ends up being struck out every time. Of course, if we are batting fourth and are expected to hit a home run, we may need to aim for one every time, but most players are expected to simply make a hit and so should focus on hitting the ball well enough to get on base.

Even if we cannot hit the ball out of the stadium, striving to hit the ball squarely every time will allow us to garner a lot of hits, producing miraculous results. Concentrating on getting the 20 percent done will no doubt bring about the other 80 percent of success.

4
20 PERCENT DECIDES THE GAME

We find the most skilled pitchers in the professional baseball leagues. They can throw fastballs as well as a variety of other pitches. Still, their records vary; some of them regularly win fifteen to twenty games a year, while others become double-digit losing pitchers every year.

A careful analysis will reveal that winning pitchers do not necessarily throw faster balls or have a greater variety of pitches. What makes them different, then? Let's look at this using the Pareto Principle. Suppose the pitcher throws one hundred balls in a game. In this case, twenty of his pitches will determine whether he will be the game's winning pitcher or the losing one. One game consists of nine innings, which means that he will throw an average of two pitches per inning that will determine whether he wins or loses. He will be a losing pitcher if those two pitches fail and a winning pitcher if they succeed. It all depends on how he does with those deciding pitches.

The pitchers who earn many wins are not the ones who can throw one hundred balls with all their might, but the ones who can concentrate on twenty balls per game, or two deciding balls per inning. The pitchers who successfully throw these two balls per inning can also gain victory over the other 80 percent of the game.

On average, a pitcher will face four to five batters per inning, but how he pitches to two of them will determine the outcome of the game. If the hitters can figure out what course the pitcher's balls will take, the pitcher will most likely allow runs. But if he can throw the type of pitches that the batter doesn't expect, he can become a winning pitcher.

I believe this is a good analogy that illustrates the principle of success in life. We spend an average of thirty to forty years of our life working, often in one career. Some people succeed at what they do, while others do not. It is true that the accumulation of our daily efforts determines how far we can progress up the ladder of success, from the entry level all the way up to the top. Still, the outcome of our success depends on how we spend the key 20 percent of our time every day. Setting our mind to score a victory in this 20 percent will ensure that we succeed at what we do.

Most people are not aware of this principle and dawdle over their work. They spend eight to ten hours every day, often repeating the same work pattern. And when they look over their life and see where they stand in the career ladder, they often feel that it was determined by the accumulation of the total work they did. But this isn't necessarily true. Their work can result in a completely different outcome if they apply the Pareto Principle to how they use their working hours.

Let's say you work from 9:00 a.m. to 7:00 p.m., which means you work ten hours a day. Think about which two hours are crucial for you to score a win for the day. Once you choose the time slot, set aside those hours to focus on producing results. Give all you've got, and concentrate all your efforts on bringing successful results in those two hours. If you work in sales, do everything you can within those two hours to achieve your sales goal for the day. If you devote those two hours to your most efficient and profitable task, you can spend the remaining eight hours doing routine work. All you have to do is make sure that you do not make any major mistakes for the rest of the day.

This principle can apply to any kind of work. Every day, set aside a period of time when you can work most efficiently, and give 100 percent of your effort to achieving results during that 20 percent of your time. In some cases, you may need to sacrifice something else to secure the 20 percent, but I still recommend that you do it, because ensuring the success of the 20 percent will bring you success in the other 80 percent of what you do for the entire day.

5
FOCUS INTENSIVELY
TO PRODUCE RESULTS

I would not be surprised if readers who know me as a prolific author think that I spend all my time each day writing books. Actually, I only use a small percentage of each month on writing. But the time I spend writing is extremely intense. I make a lot of preparations mentally, physically, and spiritually; I study a lot beforehand, get into good shape, organize my thoughts, and make sure that my mind is free of distractions.

I choose the best time of the best day, focus my attention, and write down my well-thought-through ideas with an extremely condensed mind and great enthusiasm in a short amount of time. I use the rest of my time to prepare for this intensive period, for example by reading numerous other books for reference. I also spend many hours on introspective reflection and meditation. I write only when I am in my best condition. And to be quite honest, when I finish writing, I am as exhausted as if I had just run a four-mile race.

The 80-20 rule definitely applies to how I use my time. I commit myself to doing my best work during 20 percent of my time every day and every month so that I can gain control over the other 80 percent and make the most efficient use of my time. I firmly believe that this is the key to success.

Even if you are doing office work, you can improve the quality of your time. Set aside two hours every day and use that time as efficiently as possible. Make it a fulfilling and inspiring time that lets you experience guidance from heaven. You'll be able to work on paperwork as smoothly as if you were writing automatically and speak inspirationally as if heavenly spirits are speaking through you.

If you want to think on a longer-term basis, you could focus on doing the best you can on two days out of ten. Either way, it is important to set aside a period of time when you concentrate your mind and energy to produce maximum results.

The same principle can help in our studies as well. If you just sit at your desk desultorily studying for ten hours a day, you won't make much progress. Instead, select two hours when you are in your best condition, and make that period of time as efficient as possible. Use this time frame to work on your most important studies.

The 80-20 rule also applies to reading. I've heard that some of my readers are concerned that they cannot keep up with all of the books I've published so far. But I would like to assure them that only 20 percent of the contents is essential. Let's say you are reading a 200-page book. You don't have to memorize the entire book or remember all the contents; you only need to pick out and understand about forty pages of the book that are of most importance to you. As long as you read these forty pages meticulously, you can read through the rest of the book and get the gist of what it says. Only 20 percent of the book contains pearls of wisdom that you need to grasp.

Similarly, the manuscript of this chapter runs to about fifteen pages or so, but its true essence is contained in about 20 percent, or about three pages. Once you can pick out the three pages of text that contain the most important passages in this chapter, memorize them and master them. Doing this will help you acquire a new level of understanding.

To conclude, we waste the most time at work and while studying. That's why it's crucial that we focus our time on efficiently producing results every day, so that we can make the most of our time in life.

CHAPTER 8

SETTING
our POTENTIAL
FREE

༄ 1 ༄

WE ALL FACE OBSTACLES
TO REACHING OUR POTENTIAL

"Human potential" can sound intangible, but this indefinable quality reveals how limitless our possibilities can be. Every day, I am thinking about how I can help more people bring out their hidden abilities. And I have been devoting many decades of my life and work to encouraging people to discover the extraordinary power within them.

Those of you who have been following a spiritual path for a while now may find a chapter on human potential too basic. But the truth is that fulfilling our potential is not an easy thing to do. We may believe that all we need to do is clear away negative thoughts and attune our hearts to heaven, and then we will intuitively understand the secrets of this world and the answers to our problems. But the actual journey to our hidden potential is not as easy as it may sound.

This is because we face more obstacles the further that we progress on our journey of self-betterment. When we discover deeper truths about life, we thirst for even more knowledge. The more we empathize with others' feelings, the stronger our concern for them becomes. The more we discover about our hearts and minds, the more problems we notice. These obstacles are different from the deep struggles with darkness that we all face on the path to enlightenment. They are actually just a commonplace part of our journey to a better version of us. We are meant to encounter more hurdles as we strive toward higher goals, a wider perspective, and deeper insights. We face these difficulties because our current abilities and strengths have some catching up to do if we are to meet these higher goals. This chapter is a guide for those who are always striving to be an even better version of themselves as they progress on their journey. I will show you ways to conquer the obstacles you will face whenever you take a new step toward fulfilling your potential.

～～ 2 ～～
WILLPOWER OPENS THE WAY FORWARD

W hy are we continually striving for self-betterment? There is something about continuous
growth that we value. If we tried to imagine the life
of a pebble on the beach, we would probably picture
it being washed into and away from the shore all day.
If this pebble could think, what would it think about
what it had accomplished during its days and years
drifting with the ocean's ebb and flow? What would
it say about the nature of life?

The pebble may be proud of the harmonious natural beauty it helped create. But the pebble's accomplishments can go no further than that. Because the
pebble has no volition of its own, what it is capable
of is determined by the ocean. It can move into and
out of the beach, and the occasional collision with
another pebble may erode it or shatter the other one

into pieces. But these events are just natural phe-nomena. They do not happen because the pebble desired them. The pebble's life has so little potential. The pebble is destined to keep eroding and finally diminish into a beautiful speck of sand.

We are not pebbles on the shore—we are not lim-ited to responding mechanically to external forces that buffet us about. We are the ocean, whose waves crash and recede like a creature with a will of its own. Compared with the pebble, we have extraordi-nary potential within us. We have a mind, a strong will of our own, and the ability to persevere. We determine where we go, and we can summon all the power in our possession to create a life of our own. Unlike pebbles, we can use our mind and our will-power to forge our own path forward. This potential is what makes us so remarkable.

We humans have infinite possibilities within us, and these possibilities wouldn't exist without the power of our will. Willpower is an intense energy and strong enthusiasm that is necessary to fulfill an aspiration. But strong willpower is not an inborn trait. Even though some children are naturally stronger willed or more stubborn than others, there is much more to the strength of our willpower than the personalities we started with. Inner strength is like a muscle: it can be developed and strengthened by training. Willpower is the most important part of this inner strength.

When we have a positive attitude, our will can strengthen like a muscle. It becomes powerful enough to face obstacles and flip them around, push them aside, and send them flying to clear our path forward. So if we have an aspiration that is important to human happiness—especially to our own happiness—the first step to achieving that aspiration is creating a strong will.

～ 3 ～

THE FIRST STEP TO STRONG WILLPOWER
USE DISAPPOINTMENT AS A SPRINGBOARD

What can we do to strengthen our will? The first step is to refuse to give in to defeat. The fighter within us is one of the biggest forces driving our inner strength. There is a tough spirit deep inside us that does not want to accept failure. That fighting spirit has the power to drive our will forward like a springboard.

Everyone feels a deep sense of disappointment in defeat. And this disappointment can be converted into positive energy. For example, we can use our competitive spirit to grow and learn from one another. We coexist with countless other people, and there will always be competitions between us and other people. In each of these competitions, there will always be someone who wins and someone who loses. Even though we know that no one ever wins for good or is defeated for good, a single defeat can make us heavily disappointed in ourselves.

Disappointment and feelings of inferiority in defeat are commonplace emotions for everyone. This frustration isn't necessarily a wrong emotion to have. But it is vital that we convert it into something of higher value—something more splendid, more positive, and more exalted. All the men and women we remember today as our heroes experienced defeat at some point but used their disappointment to drive them to heightened perseverance and effort toward their achievements.

No one wants to give in to defeat, so this first step is basic enough that everyone can use it to start creating strong willpower now. Of course, converting our frustration into the wrong kind of pride, denial, and over-competitiveness will develop the wrong kind of willpower. But if we can channel our frustration in a heavenly way, we can build a strong determination to better ourselves.

So if you are stuck in a rut, your enthusiasm is

low, and you want to reawaken your desire and motivation to grow, your first step is to refuse to give into defeat. Remember how able you are. Remember the possibilities you used to dream of. You don't deserve to remain disappointed and frustrated. The time has come to rally your enthusiasm so you can realize your full potential. Let yourself be inspired by the life, love, and education that you received from your parents. Be invigorated by the hopes and dreams your friends and family have for you. Ask yourself honestly: are you satisfied with where you are in life, or do you dream of more? If you stay where you are now, will you be happy, or will you have regrets? When you see someone from similar or less fortunate circumstances achieving more success than you've achieved, realize that you probably had the same number of opportunities but failed to grasp them. Let this realization spur you forward. Instead of focusing on their success, learn from your regrets, and create a strong will to improve yourself.

4

THE SECOND STEP TO STRONG WILLPOWER
REAWAKEN YOUR DREAMS

The second step to a stronger will is to have ideals. This is a more advanced way of strengthening our willpower. Our ideals are goals that we desire, deep within our hearts, to achieve. The enthusiastic pursuit of dreams is one of the most precious virtues of youth. Our youthful aspirations allow us to see the world through rose-colored glasses and believe in infinite possibilities for ourselves and the world. But over the years, we start to think less often of our ideals, and our power to follow our dreams becomes rusty.

The aim of this second step is to remember, reawaken, and cultivate our ability to dream once more. If your life is drifting, if you are struggling to break out of the status quo, or if you are trying to get somewhere but feeling stuck, you may have forgotten your dreams. No matter how young you are, if you have stopped dreaming, your heart has grown old. And if, in your forties, fifties, sixties, and even seventies, you continue to gleam with vitality and reach for your ideals, then age doesn't matter—you have the heart of youth.

If you have forgotten your ability to dream and pursue your ideals, do not fear! You can cultivate this power. The idealist within is a power we can nurture. We can keep our dreams alive by remembering them and thinking about them again as we go through our lives.

The reality of daily life in the real world erodes the grand ideals we used to dream of as children, and by the time we are in our thirties or forties, the waves of life have washed over these dreams so often they've become as tiny as a grain of sand. If that has happened to you, then this is the time to look back on your life and remember the dreams you dreamed in your youth.

Think back to when you were young, and ask

yourself: Who did you admire? What was your ideal life? What were your dreams? What got in the way of your dreams? What stopped you from holding onto your dreams and keeping them alive? Were these obstacles important enough to justify letting go of your dreams forever?

If circumstances stopped you from pursuing one of your dreams, what happened to your other dreams? Or what kept you from developing new ideals? Why did you hesitate to develop new ambitions? The answer may be that you neglected to keep dreaming. Constant effort is important, but effort is not about just laboring over hard work every day. Our effort has purpose because of the dreams that we hold dear in our hearts. So, what do your dreams mean to you now? These questions will lead you back to your real potential.

5

THE THIRD STEP TO STRONG WILLPOWER
DEDICATE YOURSELF TO THE HOLY

A devotion to a higher purpose, the wholehearted dedication of our lives to the holy, is the third step to stronger willpower. When we live for ourselves, our potential is confined by our own personal limitations, and that keeps us from accessing the extraordinary energy we are capable of. Thoughts of our own happiness cannot inspire the kind of outpouring of enthusiasm that touches people. The vigor to change the world cannot come from egoism. The power to make a difference is born of the willingness to sacrifice ourselves for a sacred purpose. We become truly strong when we use all our wisdom, power, and experience to serve the holy.

There will be situations in life when our courage will be severely tested. We will feel as though we need to be brave enough to throw ourselves over a cliff. But as the wise have said, if we discover the way in the morning, we will be free of regrets, even if we die in the evening. If our heart's desire is to dedicate our life to God, even the loss of our life leaves us nothing to regret. We can find the light of this purity of heart shining within each of us.

There is a holy energy deep inside that is waiting to be released. Throughout life, we encounter chances to set this energy free. One of these opportunities is a spiritual rebirth. From birth through childhood and into adulthood, we blindly depend on our own values. And then, one day, we come face to face with a giant wall that obstructs our path, and we become stuck. As we struggle to find a way over or around this wall, we begin to learn that we have forgotten who we really are. We start to realize that we have had a shallow comprehension of the world—perhaps that we have only followed the changing opinions of other people. We see that our old ways have led us to this wall. And by this epiphany, a crack opens in our shell of egoism, making way for our true self to reemerge. This is the moment when we are twice born. St. Paul's conversion may be the most famous of these rebirths, but each of us has our own unique experience.

We all struggle every day with all kinds of fetters that tie us down, that keep our souls from breaking free. But just think: where we live right now, where we spend our days, is just a tiny cell. It is just a small cavern. What we see around us is not the whole world. Even when we despair and lose hope in all possibility, there are times when a crack appears from above these cavernous walls and a ray of light comes shining through. This is the light of heaven.

The angels in heaven are always waiting patiently for this moment—this moment that comes after a struggle with limitations so large that we seek out heaven's help and awaken to our devotion to God. In this moment, we are invited to the greater world. It is completely new, and we gain a freedom we have never experienced before. This awakening to the spiritual self beyond the physical self brings us great strength.

～～ 6 ～～
LIVE AS IF YOU WERE IN HEAVEN
TO LIVE UP TO YOUR POTENTIAL

Each of the steps so far has been about strengthening your willpower. The final step to liberating our potential is to shift our perspective. We must open our inner eyes and perceive the world in a new way. For example, until now, your point of view may have shown you only your physical side—for example, your height and weight. But as your spiritual self awakens, your perspective shifts to a heavenly one. You begin to understand how God and the angels perceive you from their place above. You will see that this world is actually a spiritual world.

In the final analysis, following the ways of heaven is essential to our potential. The key to a remarkable life of alignment with heaven is to think of this world not as separate from the other world but as an extension of it. To live a wonderful life devoid of shame and regrets, we must live our lives as if this world were heaven, learning from all mistakes and turning them into good. This way of life gives us the power to build an ideal world on earth.

Every day is a test to help us become someone who deserves to be welcomed into heaven. No matter how severe our circumstances are, and no matter how much we want to complain and show our dissatisfaction, there is always a way to be merry, mirthful, and cheerful. This attitude will lead us to the ideal way of life.

We must discover the limitless potential of the present and explore the boundless possibilities around us. We must energize ourselves with inexhaustible cheer, no matter what our circumstances. Doing so will lead us to all answers, and all things will guide us to happiness. Happiness is not in a far off land; it can be found here and now. The ideal life we want to create is always within our grasp, no matter where we are. I hope that you will believe in this truth, and it is my hope that you will remind yourself time and again that you have the power within you to open a path to your dreams.

CHAPTER 9

CREATING
RESERVES
in LIFE

1

BREATHING ROOM IN YOUR MIND
PREVENTS NEGATIVE THINKING

We all know, somewhere in our heart, that grievance, dissatisfaction, discontent, insatiable desires, envy, and rage do not serve us in the truest sense. But we still experience these things, and we still express them. We do not want to grumble, and when we can't help but voice words of discontent, we often feel disgusted with ourselves for our lack of self-control. So in this chapter, I would like to offer precautions against the mental attitude that gives rise to negative thoughts like these. We can actually create circumstances that will prevent us from thinking negatively, and by doing so, we can save ourselves from suffering unpleasant feelings and start living a harmonious life.

How can we prevent negative thinking? Simply put, the key is to have a little breathing room in our mind. When we have inner reserves, we don't feel the need to grumble or fly into a rage. Conversely, those who are quick to anger are often narrow-minded and lose their temper easily, because they have no room in their mind.

The same holds true for jealousy. A sense of self-composure and self-confidence protects us from becoming envious of others. When we build true confidence and become more tolerant of others, we don't have to suffer from the inferiority complexes that give rise to jealousy.

Let's think about the feeling of discontent, too. When do we express frustration? It is when we feel that there is a gap or a discrepancy between our ideal self and our actual self. If our real self matches our ideal self or, better yet, if the reality we are facing is better than our ideal, then we have no reason to complain. We can dissolve feelings of discontent by improving ourselves until we surpass our ideal self. Having breathing room in our mind keeps us from harboring negative thoughts.

2

LESSONS FROM CHILDHOOD
FORM THE BASIS OF OUR LIVES

Before we go on, let's take a moment to look back in time to our childhoods, because the lessons we learn in childhood form the basis for our life, and become useful to us when we grow up.

This topic reminds me of how Japanese elementary school students spend the summer vacations. In Japan, where I grew up, the summer vacation starts in the third week of July and lasts about forty days. Since it takes place in the middle of the school year, students receive homework assignments, which they are expected to complete by the end of the vacation.

When I was a child, we would rush home on the last day of the first semester with brimming smiles, filled with joy and excitement at having the whole vacation ahead of us. Not wanting to waste a moment of free time, we would toss away our school bag and rush outside to play. But soon July would end and August would come. And before we knew it, it was August 20, ten days before the end of the summer vacation. We started to smell the first hints of autumn in the air, it gradually became cooler in the evenings, and we started to hear the insects singing at night. This was a time when a lot of Japanese kids became heavy-hearted. They started to dread their parents asking if they had finished their homework assignments, and just as they expected, their mom would soon ask how they were doing with their homework.

Those who hadn't even started any of their assignments, including time-consuming ones such as crafts and research reports, would start panicking, not knowing where to start. They felt caught in a dilemma, thinking that they would have to sacrifice some assignments to complete others or else give up on all of them. They would rack their brains frantically and cry out for help. They would ask their father to help with the craft project while asking their mother to help with other assignments.

If their father was big-hearted, he may have said, "Okay, since you have only five days left, I will help you out." But if he was not willing to help, he might have said he was too busy. Through experiences like these, some people learn at an early age that they can't depend on other people's help.

As the end of the holiday approached, they would start calling their friends, asking if they could split the homework and copy each other's work. But things would not go as they had hoped, and they would end up going through hell during the final three days of the vacation. Some of the laid-back kids would even wait till the first day of school and ask if they could copy their friends' homework then.

It is hard to start working on a homework assignment at the beginning of a vacation. Out of one hundred people, probably three could truthfully say that they always finished their homework by the end of July. When we have plenty of free time on our hands, we are tempted to take the easy way out. This may be a tendency of human beings that we cannot avoid. Even when we know that we will suffer later, we often cannot hold ourselves back from taking the bait of immediate pleasure in front of us.

A lot of people have probably gone through similar experiences when studying for exams. Students with good grades often finish their homework ahead of time and prepare themselves for the next class. Some even finish their assignments a month ahead of time or start preparing for national exams a year in advance. These are the students who do well in school. But those who cram the night before the exam or who feel the need to study after the exam are the type that likes to leave everything until the last minute. These people tend to be slow learners and develop a tendency to put things off until later. These behaviors represent the person's pattern of thoughts, which form our perspective of life and often determine our outlook for the future.

In an Aesop's fable "The Tortoise and the Hare," the slow and steady tortoise wins the race against the swift hare. You certainly don't have to spend your whole life rushing around like a hare, and there's a lesson we can learn from the tortoise type of life style. But the hare who leaves the tortoise far behind and takes a nap in the middle of the race can also teach us a lesson—at the very least, it is impressive that the hare managed to get so far ahead that it had enough time to take a nap.

When we fret and worry, it is usually over issues at hand or in the near future. We usually don't worry about what may happen in the distant future. Someone who is worried about something that may happen several decades from now is either a person of high caliber or an extremely nervous person. In most cases, our worries concern things that we are facing now or things that may happen in the next few weeks or within a year at the longest.

If you feel that you have a tendency to think negatively, it's a good idea to go against common wisdom and start living like a hare. At the very least, the hare who is focused on getting far enough ahead to have time for a nap is probably free from worry.

Do you find yourself putting things off until the last minute? Are you the type who starts working on your assignment right before the deadline or who feels that you are always behind others? If your answers to these questions are "yes," I'm sure the perspective of the hare will help you make new discoveries.

⌒ 3 ⌒
PREPARING FOR LIFE IN ADVANCE

My point in telling these stories is to show you another way of creating space in your mind. Fast-forwarding your life and preparing yourself for what's to come allows you to rid yourself of distress over issues that may come up in a month, three months, or six months. Instead of waiting until the last minute, we can get a head start on the things we need to do, and this head start will give us more room in our mind.

Let's say you are supposed to prepare three meals each day. You don't have to wait until an hour before the meal to start cooking. As you cook dinner, for example, you can simultaneously start preparing for lunch the next day. You can certainly do this, unless you are cooking food that goes bad quickly. If you need to peel and slice vegetables for dinner, you might as well precook the vegetables for lunch the following day. Or better yet, if you plan menus for the entire week, you can buy all the ingredients and prepare them more efficiently.

Consider yourself objectively: Are you the type who would panic and hastily prepare lunch just before noon and then realize at five o'clock in the evening that you need to get started on dinner right away? Or do you think you are wise enough to plan menus for the following day or even the coming week?

If you are the first type, do you find yourself losing your cool when something unexpected happens? For instance, do you get upset when your children bring up issues when you're in a hurry to prepare lunch? If you get an unexpected visitor, does it ruin your schedule for the entire day? Do you go out to get groceries for dinner without any plan about what to buy? Perhaps you simply buy things that catch your eye, but when you go home, you realize that you forgot to buy something and need to make a second trip to the store. People of the first type might repeat this kind of behavioral pattern over and over.

But the latter type, who can plan meals for tomorrow, can also be more efficient in their tasks for today. If they can plan for the entire week in advance, it will shift how they approach today and tomorrow. But I believe that not many people fit this description; instead, many people today are unprepared for what they will face in the future.

Let's consider another situation in which it pays to prepare for the future. Let's say you are an unhappy wife who moans how untidy your husband is. When your husband comes home from work, he leaves his dirty clothes on the floor. He leaves everything in a mess. It is like having another three-year-old in the house; you have to follow him around and clean up the mess he leaves behind. It gives you a headache just to watch him. It makes you sweat or shiver just imagining how much work you're going to have to do to clean up the mess he's making.

Now, let's think about how you might plan ahead

to preempt this situation. The first step is to watch his behavioral patterns and analyze his habits. We can easily guess what part of the pond carp will be swimming in a few minutes from now, because they form a group and head in a certain direction. Similarly, your husband probably has set habits that can allow you to guess what he will do after he comes home. Once you know his behavioral pattern, you can take preemptive action against it.

When he arrives home, before he does anything, tell him specifically what he needs to do. You can tell him to change his clothes in a specific area and to leave his dirty clothes in a particular spot; you can specify where he should hang his suit and tie. Let him follow and repeat this new pattern of behavior until it becomes his new habit. For instance, if he has a habit of taking his clothes off in the living room and leaving his dirty clothes there, you can train him to take them off in the laundry room. This will free you from forever clearing up after him and erase your stress.

Let's look at another example. Say you're a mother whose kids always moan that they can't finish their homework in time. Even if they are given the homework well in advance, you can easily foresee that they will run out of time, because you yourself probably faced the same problem when you were their age. It is very common for kids to put off their homework until the last minute and then make a fuss about how they won't be able to finish it before the deadline. You can plan ahead and make preemptive action against this, too. If they receive a homework assignment a month in advance of the deadline, tell them that you will take them on a trip, to a theme park, or to the beach as a reward for finishing all their homework within ten days. In this way, you can make sure that they finish their homework well in advance. Making this kind of behavior a habit can avoid any commotion that they may make right before the due date, letting you keep your composure and live more peacefully.

~ 4 ~
ESTABLISHING FINANCIAL STABILITY

You can use this same strategy in many other aspects of life. Let's consider how we can apply it to our household finances.

Do you ever get restless before payday because you have used up your last paycheck? I'm sure a lot of people have experienced this. Just before payday, they get pinched for money and hardly have enough to buy food. But as soon as the money comes in, they loosen their purse strings and start spending money without considering what will happen at the end of the month. If you find yourself repeating this pattern of behavior month after month, perhaps you need to think ahead and plan how you are going to spend and save the money you earn.

Among the books I read in my younger days, the works of Dr. Seiroku Honda (1866–1952) left a profound mark on me. Dr. Honda was a university professor and landscape architect, active during the pre- and post-World War II periods, whose works include *The Secret to My Success in Life.** He practiced what he called the "25 percent deduction method" which helped him become one of the top income earners in Japan, even though his salary at the University of Tokyo was not exceptionally high. He was even commended by the tax office for paying the highest income tax. Not only was he known for his financial success, he was also very active and recognized for his achievements and contributions to society. He made nineteen trips overseas, an astonishing number considering the situation before World War II in Japan, when international travel was very rare among ordinary citizens. He also published well over three hundred books.

After he graduated from college, Honda went to Germany to study, where one of his professors

---

* This title is an English translation of the Japanese title. This book is only available in Japanese. The original title is *Waga Shosei No Hiketsu*, published by Jitsugyo no Nihon Sha, Ltd., in July 1978 in Tokyo, Japan.

repeatedly taught him that if he wanted to devote his life to study, he would need to build a solid financial footing. His professor told him that the main reason scholars have to discontinue their studies is a lack of funds. Without sufficient money to buy books or pay for a space or room to store their books, scholars had to start living modestly, which limited their opportunity to pursue their studies. The professor advised Honda to improve his financial situation after he returned to Japan and to create a life plan to accumulate wealth, because his savings would be the key to the development of his academic life.

Upon returning to Japan, Honda dedicated himself to carrying out the professor's advice. The basic method he employed to accumulate wealth was to save 25 percent of his income. He was so determined that when he ran out of money toward the end of the month, he got his family's consent to survive on rice alone so that he could put aside the money as savings. He deposited any extra money that came in, such as bonuses or unexpected income, into his savings account, and when his savings reached a certain amount, he invested it wisely. Gradually his unearned income outstripped his salary. This is how Honda built a very strong financial base.

I've never heard of any University of Tokyo professors, other than Dr. Honda, who were ranked among the top earners in the country. This shows how thoroughly he followed his plan to create a stable financial base.

If you wish to gain economic wealth, you have to start by saving. People today tend to prioritize consumption over saving. They even buy things they can't afford, thinking that they will pay later, when money comes in. This happens when the rational mind is overcome by desire. Purchasing something in anticipation of extra income in the future leads to a financially hellish life. Many businesses and stores take advantage of this lifestyle and encourage people to buy now and pay later or pay back in installments, giving rise to a debt-oriented economy.

The basic rule for leading a financially stable life

is to live within our means. And if we want to lead a financially heavenly life, we should save a certain percentage of our income. This basic principle holds true in every era, regardless of how advanced our economic structure becomes. Saving money and leaving sufficient funds for the future make us feel at ease.

Even if someone tells you how convenient their credit system is or how much you will save on taxes in the end, if you owe a debt, it means that you are creating negative earnings, which you will have to work to pay back. The collateral you are pledging is your future labor that you have yet to undertake. You will inevitably feel uneasy about the future; you will be assailed by mounting anxiety about maintaining your health and your ability to continue working. You will work restlessly, as if goaded by your debt. Some people say that they are not motivated to work unless they have a debt to pay off, but this kind of mindset keeps us away from achieving great success.

If we want to become rich, we need to save money. No matter how much we earn, if we spend it all, we will be left with no money in the end. Living within the limits of our earnings and putting aside a certain amount each month in savings—this basic principle for accumulating wealth applies to everyone, regardless of their occupation. Saving money for the future while leading a frugal lifestyle within our means is the path to prosperity.

❦ 5 ❦

CREATING RESERVES FOR THE FUTURE

C reating reserves for the future works in exactly the same way as saving money. As we develop the habit of accumulating wealth, we can apply these techniques to our work and other aspects of life. What's important is the general principle: preparing ahead of time for what we know we will need in the future.

To create any kind of reserve for the future, we simply take whatever extra time, money, and ideas we have at the moment and use them in a way that will bring future returns. Developing a mental habit of investing our resources in something that will bring us profits is essential for creating reserves in life.

If we are raising children, for example, we should consider what will happen six months from now, one year from now, or even further into the future. Then we can make plans considering the relationship between the household's finances and children's upbringing.

The same can be said about learning the Truths. Rushing through our studies as if to meet a deadline will not help us achieve enlightenment any faster. Enlightenment can only be attained by making steady, step-by-step progress.

In maintaining our health too, we should take precautions against getting sick, instead of waiting until we are struck with a serious illness to go to a doctor. There are only two ways to keep from falling sick. One way is to build physical strength, and the other is to take ample rest so we never completely exhaust ourselves. But many people today cannot adopt these simple practices. They keep working until they fall sick, or they immerse themselves in leisure activity until they get tired out. They don't think about taking a rest until they fall ill.

We can't underestimate the importance of rest.

A major cause of much of our distress is physical or mental exhaustion. Probably 80 percent of our worries disappear when we are rested. Preventing fatigue is a very effective protective measure against distress. Many people do not know how to relax mentally; they neglect taking care of themselves and don't take the rest they need. These people often overwork themselves until they are on the verge of a breakdown. But resting as a precaution is the secret to a long and active life.

There are techniques to avoid getting tired out. One is to break down a difficult task into smaller parts and work on it step by step. If you are constantly very busy because you have many tasks that you need to handle, try sorting them in order of importance. Then focus more energy on the most important tasks and place less emphasis on the peripheral ones. Giving everything you've got to every single task may sound ideal, but you won't be able to keep working like that forever.

The key is to create reserves in our life. There are

many ways to do this, but making preparations well in advance is the basis of all of them. It all comes down to preparing for your life ahead of time.

The first step for living a life with reserves is to have the right mindset. When we make up our mind to prepare well in advance for what we will face in our life, it becomes easier to come up with specific ideas and strategies for doing so as we need them.

Creating reserves in our life lets us live a life of contentment, a life without grievance and dissatisfaction. We can live free from rage and envy. This is the kind of heavenly life I wish for us all to lead.

CHAPTER 10

LIVING *with* VITALITY *and* HEALTH

❦ 1 ❦

THE FIRST KEY

TAKE RESPONSIBILITY FOR YOUR HEALTH

Health and vitality are so important to our lives. Life has many problems and adversities that we need to face, and we are often besieged by other people's negative thinking. But when we can encounter these problems with good health, we have a strong foundation for solving them. And what's more, good health can actually prevent many of these difficulties from arising in the first place.

Your own experience probably tells you that people who have few problems to deal with are strong, healthy, and always full of vitality. On the other hand, you can imagine that people with a weak constitution struggle with many problems. These are the chronic worriers who tend to keep producing problems for themselves. People like this are often troubled by a delicate stomach, persistent anxiety, and wrinkles between the eyebrows. We all want to avoid this type of life.

Instead, we would rather have a strong body and a mind that is relaxed, open, and invigorated by positive thinking. So the first key to a life of health and vitality is appreciating how much of a difference keeping ourselves healthy makes in the quality of our lives. Maintaining our health is so important because, if we put it off for too long, we may have to pay a high price for our neglect. I think of taking care of our health as a journey on a train. To ride the train, we need to purchase a ticket in advance, because we won't be allowed on without one. Our bodies work the same way. Our physical bodies are our souls' means of transportation through this world. For us to make it to the end of this journey, we need to fuel and maintain our bodies before they start wearing out.

The longer we put off doing this, the higher the price becomes. If we wait until we reach our destination to pay for the ride, we will probably have to pay more than we would have if we had paid right before boarding. The same thing happens with our health: we will have to pay a higher price if we wait too long to take care of it. Since most of us are born completely healthy at birth and are taken care of by our parents for many years, our bodies have begun the journey with a good healthy start. But as soon as we become independent, the responsibility for our health falls on us. That means that when we become adults, we need to know how long we want our journey to last.

You may want this life to last until you're at least seventy. Or you may dream of living to one hundred. If you choose a lifespan of seventy years, this may be the equivalent of traveling 70,000 miles by rail. And if you prefer a lifespan of one hundred years, this may be like a journey of 100,000 miles by rail. Either way, traveling long distances like these obviously requires a good deal of preparation ahead of time. And making our health last through the decades requires the same thing. To make the journey of lifelong health and longevity, we need to put a lot of effort into preparing our bodies.

2

THE SECOND KEY

BEGIN DEVELOPING HEALTHY HABITS NOW

The second step to good health is to start taking care of your health early, before you get out of shape. It is common for people to keep putting off exercise until their circumstances show that they can't ignore their issues anymore. But by the time the doctor discovers problems with our health, a lot of damage has already been done. And when our bodies start to show warning signs that our stamina is diminishing, we have a lot of catching up to do.

The key is to understand that our bodies work like our savings account. We create a savings account to financially prepare for important plans in the future. So for our bodies to be ready for bigger, more important work in the future, we need to prepare our health ahead of time, too. Even though we may be strong and fit enough for the work we do now, we will need far more strength in the future as our work grows.

So how do we start preparing? This may sound counterintuitive, but we strengthen our mind and body by doing things that are the opposite of the type of work we do for a living. For example, if you make a living as a writer or a speaker, the nature of your work is intellectually intensive. So to revitalize your intellectual acuity, you won't need additional hours of reading. Instead, you will need physical exercise. Our minds were designed to become more vigorous when our body is strengthened.

If you haven't been getting around to reading the books on your nightstand because of bad eyesight or because your mind doesn't feel sharp enough, an accumulation of physical fatigue may be the real reason behind it. Your body may be running on an energy deficit every day, and this could be making you tired. If you were on a bus and the person sitting next to you were coughing, would you feel as if you might catch a cold at any minute? If you would, this is a sign that your body has become significantly weakened and that you need to develop a healthier lifestyle. It isn't healthy to feel vulnerable to diseases. Instead, we want to be so positive and healthy that we'd shine with an aura of vitality even if we were surrounded by coughing people. This would be the ideal life.

My work is intellectually intensive, and in my personal experience, increasing my muscular strength significantly boosted my mental acuity. As my arms and legs grew stronger, my intellectual vigor was also revitalized. This probably happened because physical strength helps prevent fatigue.

It is common for people in intellectual fields of work to have weaker stamina and for people in physically intensive jobs to have weaker mental acuity. We are inclined toward one or the other, by and large. But developing both at the same time isn't a good solution either. This usually results in mediocrity. So what is the best way of building vitality without compromising our career success? If our job is chiefly intellectual, the key is to fit exercise into our free time to build our strength. The aim isn't to become as fit as people who have physically intensive jobs. What we want to do is create the habit of regularly exercising for a set amount of time. To keep our immune systems healthy enough to protect us against illnesses, working out once a week is the bare minimum. Increasing our workouts to twice a week is enough to sustain an above-average level of stamina. And increasing them to three times a week or more will develop you into a consistent positive thinker.

Being physically fit is essential to our ability to think positively, especially when we face the stress of large and important projects. In situations in which we might think negatively or shrink from difficulties if we are tired, being fit helps us see our circumstances in a positive light. We've all been in a situation in which we were so tired that our imagination kept conjuring up mistakes and disasters that might happen. When we're exhausted, it is really difficult to get out of this negative mental loop, and this is sometimes the cause of missed opportunities for success. In times like these, well-maintained stamina becomes our greatest ally.

Developing physical vitality is essential to paving the way to our future. When I had a career in a trading company, my goal was to develop my intellect. So I allotted a large budget to books. But I became easily fatigued, and my health weakened significantly. When I began a new life as a speaker to follow my dream of spreading happiness, I realized that strong health was going to be essential to my work. Since then, I have routinely increased my level of exercise as my days have become busier. I have surprised many people by telling them that it's my habit to add intense workouts whenever my schedule becomes packed with weekly speaking engagements or when I have talks scheduled within two or three days of each other. Most people expect that intensifying your exercise during a busy schedule will end up exhausting you even more. But I have been following this method for a long time, and it has never failed me. I always get positive results from this habit.

Since we all are generally inclined to invest in either our intellectual growth or our physical maintenance but not both, the secret to a successful career is to build one or the other as your primary lifestyle and then begin incorporating the other to make further progress. This is the key to a good life.

3

THE THIRD KEY

INVEST 10 PERCENT OF YOUR INCOME IN EXERCISE

The first thing we need to take care of our health may come as a surprise for religious enthusiasts: money. Financial investment in our health is essential. If you have any hesitation about spending money on your health, start thinking of it as a wise investment rather than a waste. Maintaining our health gives us consistent energy to run our bodies, like the coal or electricity that fuels a train. Scrimping on this energy source now will end up costing us much more down the road. We need to realize that maintaining our health is a necessary expense.

That means that you need to ask yourself this question: so far, how much of your monthly income have you been spending on improving your health? I begin with this question because I commonly find that people don't hesitate to spend money on their social life but rarely give thought to spending money on their health. This may sound familiar to city-dwelling businesspeople. We rise early in the morning, work long hours, and come home late at night, frequently after a few drinks with colleagues. We all know that this kind of lifestyle puts a lot of strain on our bodies. But it is hard to turn down social engagements, and we end up watching as the pounds keep piling on.

This brings up another common habit: we often think about how much exercise we were or weren't able to fit into our week, but we don't think of the things that can help us sustain regular exercise with a little investment. If you haven't yet thought of investing money in your health, I recommend it: it is a good way to start taking better care of your health. Allowing ourselves a budget for health opens up an array of possibilities that can help us get regular exercise.

For example, if our monthly income is three thousand dollars, setting aside just 10 percent will give us three hundred dollars. This is plenty of money to allow for a dance or swimming class or a monthly membership at the local gym or country club. These kinds of activities help keep exercise interesting and so motivate us to keep doing it. For that reason, you have a better chance of staying consistent with your exercise if you invest money on a monthly basis in a form of exercise you enjoy. So if there is room in your budget, I strongly recommend making this investment.

Of course, not all of us need exercise. Some of us have physically intensive jobs that keep us in good shape. In this case, we may instead want to invest 10 percent of our income in physical rest or relaxation. Treating ourselves to a good dinner may be another way to spend our health budget. But for the rest of us, who don't get physical exercise from our jobs, it's important to regularly invest a fixed part of our income in building a healthy life.

4

THE FOURTH KEY
INVEST EXTRA TIME IN EXERCISE
IF YOU CAN'T INVEST MONEY

Of course, for some of us, there just isn't any room in our finances to do that. Don't worry—there are ways to make up for a lack of a budget. If we can't spend money, we always have the alternative option of spending our time. For example, if we can't pay for a membership at a sports club, we can instead fit in more hours of exercise by waking up thirty minutes earlier on weekdays or setting aside some time on weekends. This won't require any money at all.

Some kinds of exercise cost virtually nothing—for example, walking, jogging, and running. These less-expensive exercises are often the most effective in getting us into shape, if we can stick with them. In addition, there are exercises that use equipment that may be more interesting and so more sustainable—

for example, jump-roping, practicing bat swings, and practicing golf swings. These low-cost exercises can feel drab and so be difficult to sustain, so a good tip is to set up a buddy system with a friend or family member. An exercise buddy helps keep things interesting, and the support keeps us from getting derailed from our exercise goals. Make a commitment with a friend or family member to exercise together regularly for a set amount of time, share your progress with each other, and give each other support.

5

THE FIFTH KEY
REST AND TAKE BREAKS
TO PREVENT FATIGUE

The last key for lifelong health and vitality is preventing fatigue. Creating a lifestyle that keeps us from building fatigue deserves special attention, because it is vital to eliminating many of the problems we go through. As I mentioned in the previous chapter, many of our problems are small enough to solve quickly. When we have the kind of vitality that wakes us up feeling reinvigorated and enables us to enjoy a good breakfast in the morning, we quickly find solutions to most problems. But if we have a hard time getting out of bed and making breakfast and we tend to be moody around others, many of the problems that come up will appear more difficult than they really are. Even small issues will seem impossible to deal with, just because we are tired.

There are several things we can do to prevent

fatigue. They are based on the principle that regular rest makes the body more efficient. First, we need to keep in mind, while we are working, that our concentration doesn't last longer than an hour. It lasts two to three hours at best. If we work any longer than that, we'll notice ourselves rapidly losing focus.

Many office jobs these days require spending such long hours at a desk from morning to night that our productivity is guaranteed to suffer. Some businesspeople get to the office at 8:00 in the morning and head home at 9:00 or 10:00 in the evening. That is an average of twelve hours a day at a desk. It is impossible for anyone to keep concentrating for such a long span of time. If we try, our productivity will fall, and we will waste a lot of time.

One way to keep our concentration going is to take a ten- or fifteen-minute break for every two to three hours of work or, preferably, every hour. I recommend taking at least five minutes to relax your mind after every fifty-five minutes of focused work. Mornings are often not a problem, since we are the most alert during these hours. So the challenge starts after lunch. Some people like to keep pushing themselves and won't slow down at all. But I recommend that everyone take breaks seriously. Even if a ten-minute break seems like a waste of time, it will be worth it in the end. When we don't take breaks but instead try to push ourselves through the hours, our productivity suffers so much that those hours end up going to waste anyway. So incorporating ten- to fifteen-minute breaks will do us tremendous good down the road.

These breaks have an important purpose: relaxation. During your breaks, purposefully develop the habit of unwinding your mind. You could have some coffee or tea to help you release tension. Or you might enjoy a chitchat with your colleagues. Even better is to throw some humor into these conversations.

Next, make sure to do your most important work during the hours of your peak performance. Don't wait until 6:00 to work on the most important jobs. Tiredness sets in during the evening, so this is the worst time of day to work on your most important projects. Waiting that late usually means delivering lower-quality work. It is key to plan your day so that you are doing your most important jobs when you are feeling your best. If you absolutely need to work in the evening, I recommend setting aside mechanical tasks such as filing for those hours.

I also recommend giving your body a chance to lie down. Take advantage of a sofa if one is available. I recommend this because our lower back and feet are vital to keeping us going through extended hours of work. A weakened lower back often results in diminished stamina and loss of concentration. By giving your body a chance to lie down, your lower back will have an opportunity to relax and relieve tension. Stretching is also a good way to release muscle tension.

Lying down is also great for our feet. Our feet need a chance to rest, too. They work hard to support our entire body weight on a small surface area. We usually spend at least several hours on our feet throughout the day, but it puts a lot of strain on our feet to stay standing for more than an hour at a time. It does a lot of good for our body to mindfully give our feet some relief from our weight.

Finally, our eyes are also an important part of our body, and we need to care for them. It's hard to avoid at least some eyestrain, because of the work we put our eyes through. But tired eyes have negative effects on our ability to think and can even cause weak digestion, anxiety, and feelings of victimization. So what can we do to take care of our eyes? First, we can work in good lighting with a constant level of brightness. We should also keep our eyes eight inches away from the paper or screen we are looking at. In addition, we should avoid small typefaces. When you purchase books, it is always a good idea to look for a version with a bigger typeface, if one is available, even if it costs a few extra dollars. This is why IRH Press publishes our books with large fonts and generous layouts—because we want to help our readers keep their eyes healthy.

Giving our eyes regular breaks is another important way of taking care of them. Resting our eyes is as important as resting our lower back and feet. A simple method to relax your eyes is to look at something else. Looking away from your paper or screen after a period of work will give your eyes some relief. It puts a lot of strain on them to keep them focused for five to ten continuous hours. But they will be able to work throughout the day as long as you give them breaks. So, as with our lower back and feet, our eyes also need a few minutes to relax every hour.

Everyone with intellectual pursuits will eventually face problems with their eyesight, so to be sure that we can keep using them for many years, it is important to keep looking for ways of taking good care of them. I hope that the tips in this section will help everyone take good care of their lower back, feet, and eyes to prevent fatigue from building up.

AFTERWORD TO THE ORIGINAL EDITION

It was my pleasure to write a book about the heart of work, and I would like to explain how it came about. I was inspired to write this book when I learned that chapter 5 was well-received by my readers when it was first published in the Japanese version of Happy Science Monthly. This made me think about what work must mean to our lives, and I realized how important it is to share my views on how we—especially those with spiritual values—should think of work.

So I wrote about my philosophy of work to develop my answer. We could think of our work and the heart separately—and I am sure that many people do—but I see them as inseparable parts of our lives. Our inner world and our work are the same things, just expressed in different forms. This view of work became the foundation of my work philosophy.

What I wrote developed into chapters 1 through 4, and I compiled chapters 5 through 10 from a six-part series that was printed in the July to December issues in 1989 of Happy Science Monthly, where chapter 5 had originally appeared.

I hope that this book will be well-loved throughout your life, and I will also write more books about my philosophy of work. It is my wish that within this book, many readers will find inspirations for new business philosophies for the coming age.

Ryuho Okawa
Founder and CEO
Happy Science Group

ABOUT THE AUTHOR

Ryuho Okawa is a renowned spiritual thinker, leader, and author in Japan with a simple goal: to help people find true happiness and create a better world. To date, Okawa's books have sold over 100 million copies worldwide and been translated into 28 languages. His books address vital issues such as how our thoughts influence reality, the nature of love, and the path to enlightenment.

In 1986, Okawa founded Happy Science as a spiritual movement dedicated to bringing greater happiness to humankind by uniting religions and cultures to live in harmony. Happy Science has grown rapidly from its beginnings in Japan to a worldwide organization. The spiritual workshops Happy Science offers are open to people of all faiths and walks of life and are rooted in the same simple principles of happiness that inspired Okawa's own spiritual awakening. Okawa is compassionately committed to the spiritual growth of others; in addition to writing and publishing books, he continues to give talks around the world.

ABOUT HAPPY SCIENCE

Happy Science is a global movement that empowers individuals to find purpose and spiritual happiness and to share that happiness with their families, societies, and the world. With more than twelve million members around the world, Happy Science aims to increase awareness of spiritual truths and expand our capacity for love, compassion, and joy so that together we can create the kind of world we all wish to live in.

Activities at Happy Science are based on the Principles of Happiness (Love, Wisdom, Self-Reflection, and Progress). These principles embrace worldwide philosophies and beliefs, transcending boundaries of culture and religions.

Love teaches us to give ourselves freely without expecting anything in return; it encompasses giving, nurturing, and forgiveness.

Wisdom leads us to the insights of spiritual truths, and opens us to the true meaning of life and the will of God (the universe, the highest power, Buddha).

Self-Reflection brings a mindful, nonjudgmental lens to our thoughts and actions to help us find our truest selves—the essence of our souls—and deepen our connection to the highest power. It helps us attain a clean and peaceful mind and leads us to the right life path.

Progress emphasizes the positive, dynamic aspects of our spiritual growth—actions we can take to manifest and spread happiness around the world. It's a path that not only expands our soul growth, but also furthers the collective potential of the world we live in.

PROGRAMS AND EVENTS

The doors of Happy Science are open to all. We offer a variety of programs and events, including self-exploration and self-growth programs, spiritual seminars, meditation and contemplation sessions, study groups, and book events.

Our programs are designed to:

- Deepen your understanding of your purpose and meaning in life
- Improve your relationships and increase your capacity to love unconditionally
- Attain a peace of mind, decrease anxiety and stress, and feel positive
- Gain deeper insights and broader perspective on the world
- Learn how to overcome life's challenges
  ... and much more.

For more information, visit our website at happyscience-na.org or happy-science.org.

INTERNATIONAL SEMINARS

Each year, friends from all over the world join our international seminars, held at our faith centers in Japan. Different programs are offered each year and cover a wide variety of topics, including improving relationships, practicing the Eightfold Path to enlightenment, and loving yourself, to name just a few.

HAPPY SCIENCE MONTHLY

Our monthly publication covers the latest featured lectures, members' life-changing experiences and other news from members around the world, book reviews, and many other topics. Downloadable PDF files are available at happyscience-na.org. Copies and back issues in Portuguese, Chinese, and other languages are available upon request. For more information, contact us via e-mail at tokyo@happy-science.org.

CONTACT INFORMATION

Happy Science is a worldwide organization with faith centers around the globe. For a comprehensive list of centers, visit the worldwide directory at happy-science. org or happyscience-na.org. The following are some of the many Happy Science locations:

United States and Canada

New York
79 Franklin Street
New York, NY 10013
Phone: 212-343-7972
Fax: 212-343-7973
Email: ny@happy-science.org
website: newyork.happyscience-na.org

Los Angeles
1590 E. Del Mar Blvd.
Pasadena, CA 91106
Phone: 626-395-7775
Fax: 626-395-7776
Email: la@happy-science.org
website: losangeles.happyscience-na.org

Orange County
10231 Slater Ave #204
Fountain Valley, CA 92708
Phone: 714-745-1140
Email: oc@happy-science.org

San Diego
Email: sandiego@happy-science.org

San Francisco
525 Clinton Street
Redwood City, CA 94062
Phone/Fax: 650-363-2777
Email: sf@happy-science.org
website: sanfrancisco.happyscience-na.org

Florida
12208 N 56th St.,
Temple Terrace, FL 33617
Phone:813-914-7771
Fax: 813-914-7710
Email: florida@happy-science.org
website: florida.happyscience-na.org

New Jersey
725 River Rd. #102B
Edgewater, NJ 07025
Phone: 201-313-0127
Fax: 201-313-0120
Email: nj@happy-science.org
website: newjersey.happyscience-na.org

Atlanta

1874 Piedmont Ave. NE
Suite 360-C
Atlanta, GA 30324
Phone: 404-892-7770
Email: atlanta@happy-science.org
website: atlanta.happyscience-na.org

Hawaii

1221 Kapiolani Blvd., Suite 920
Honolulu, HI 96814
Phone: 808-591-9772
Fax: 808-591-9776
Email: hi@happy-science.org
website: hawaii.happyscience-na.org

Kauai

4504 Kukui Street
Dragon Building Suite 21
Kapaa, HI 96746
Phone: 808-822-7007
Fax: 808-822-6007
Email: kauai-hi@happy-science.org
website: happyscience-kauai.org

Toronto

323 College Street,
Toronto, ON M5T 1S2
Canada
Phone/Fax: 1-416-901-3747
Email: toronto@happy-science.org
website: happyscience-na.org

Vancouver

#212-2609 East 49th Avenue
Vancouver, V5S 1J9
Canada
Phone: 1-604-437-7735
Fax: 1-604-437-7764
Email: vancouver@happy-science.org
website: happyscience-na.org

International

Tokyo

1-6-7 Togoshi
Shinagawa, Tokyo, 142-0041
Japan
Phone: 81-3-6384-5770
Fax: 81-3-6384-5776
Email: tokyo@happy-science.org
website: happy-science.org

London

3 Margaret Street,
London, W1W 8RE
United Kingdom
Phone: 44-20-7323-9255
Fax: 44-20-7323-9344
Email: eu@happy-science.org
website: happyscience-uk.org

Sydney

516 Pacific Hwy
Lane Cove North,
2066 NSW
Australia
Phone: 61-2-9411-2877
Fax: 61-2-9411-2822
Email: aus@happy-science.org
website: happyscience.org.au

Brazil Headquarters

Rua. Domingos de Morais 1154,
Vila Mariana, Sao Paulo,
CEP 04009-002
Brazil
Phone: 55-11-5088-3800
Fax: 55-11-5088-3806
Email: sp@happy-science.org
website: cienciadafelicidade.com.br

Jundiai

Rua Congo, 447,
Jd.Bonfiglioli,Jundiai- CEP 13207 - 340
Phone: 55-11-4587-5952
Email: jundiai@happy-sciece.org

Seoul

74, Sadang-ro 27-gil,
Dongjak-gu, Seoul, Korea
Phone: 82-2-3478-8777
Fax: 82-2-3478-9777
Email: korea@happy-science.org
website: happyscience-korea.org

Taipei

No. 89, Lane 155, Dunhua N. Road
Songshan District
Taipei City 105
Taiwan
Phone: 886-2-2719-9377
Fax: 886-2-2719-5570
Email: taiwan@happy-science.org
website: happyscience-tw.org

Malaysia

No 22A, Block2, Jalil Link
Jalan Jalil Jaya 2, Bukit Jalil
57000, Kuala Lumpur
Malaysia
Phone: 60-3-8998-7877
Fax: 60-3-8998-7977
Email: Malaysia@happy-science.org
Website: happyscience.org.my

Kathmandu

Kathmandu Metropolitan City,
Ward No. 15, Ring Road, Kimdol,
Sitapaila,Kathmandu
Nepal
Phone: 97-714-272931
Email: nepal@happy-science.org
        nepaltrainingcenter@happy-
            science.org

Uganda

Plot 877 Rubaga Road Kampala
P.O. Box 34130
Kampala, Uganda
Phone: 256-79-3238-002
Email: uganda@happy-science.org

About IRH Press USA

IRH Press USA Inc. was founded in 2013 as an affiliated firm of IRH Press Co., Ltd. Based in New York, the press publishes books in various categories including spirituality, religion, and self-improvement, and publishes books by Ryuho Okawa, the author of 100 million books sold worldwide. For more information, visit OkawaBooks.com.

You can follow Ryuho Okawa and his latest book releases at Goodreads, Facebook and Twitter

BOOKS BY RYUHO OKAWA

THINK BIG!
Be Positive and Be Brave to Achieve Your Dreams

INVITATION TO HAPPINESS
7 Inspirations from Your Inner Angel

MESSAGES FROM HEAVEN
What Jesus, Buddha, Muhammad, and Moses Would Say Today

THE LAWS OF THE SUN
One Source, One Planet, One People

CHANGE YOUR LIFE, CHANGE THE WORLD
A Spiritual Guide to Living Now

THE MOMENT OF TRUTH
Become a Living Angel Today

THE NINE DIMENSIONS
Unveiling the Laws of Eternity

SECRETS OF THE EVERLASTING TRUTHS
A New Paradigm for Living on Earth

For a complete list of books, visit OkawaBooks.com.